YOUR SCORE

"Anthony Davenport has put together the most thorough and easy-to-understand book about credit scores. If you are like most people and are baffled by what a credit score is and how it can affect your life, this is the book for you."

— Chaka Pilgrim, executive, Roc Nation

"This is a masterful work. In making the broad and complex world of personal finance so accessible and interesting, Anthony Davenport has produced a book that is remarkably helpful to all who are affected by the subject (which is everyone). The time it takes to read this book will produce extraordinary returns, both in the moment and over a lifetime."

— Mark Gerson, chairman, Gerson Lehrman Group

"*Your Score* does a phenomenal job of pulling back the curtain and giving you a firsthand peek inside the hidden, often frustrating world of credit scoring. Even better: Anthony Davenport tells you exactly how to navigate this complex system so you get the high credit score you want."

— Lynnette Khalfani-Cox, author of *Perfect Credit* and the *New York Times* bestseller *Zero Debt: The Ultimate Guide to Financial Freedom*

"Davenport offers a handy, one-stop guide to understanding—and fixing—your credit score. Outraged at practices he found predatory and nontransparent, Davenport left the industry to instead provide credit-management services. He brings both sides of his expertise to answering common credit-related questions. Credit is undeniably big business, and in Davenport's eyes, it's also a creepy one, wherein credit bureaus and consumers have an inherently adversarial and imbalanced relationship; credit bureaus, he posits, want customers to think their scores are complicated, but anyone can learn how they work. His offering is a step-by-step manual to understanding your 'real' financial score, not the estimate provided by free annual reports. He guides readers through identifying and fixing common mistakes, making sense of the report itself, and building a strong credit profile . . . Davenport has written a clearheaded, must-read guide for anyone looking to decode the most influential number of them all."

—*Publishers Weekly*

YOUR SCORE

YOUR SCORE

An Insider's Secrets to Understanding, Controlling, and Protecting Your Credit Score

ANTHONY DAVENPORT

with Matthew Rudy

Mariner Books
Houghton Mifflin Harcourt
Boston   New York

First Mariner Books edition 2019

Library of Congress Cataloging-in-Publication Data
Names: Davenport, Anthony, author.
Title: Your score : an insider's secrets to understanding, controlling, and
protecting your credit score / Anthony Davenport with Matthew Rudy.
Description: Boston : Houghton Mifflin Harcourt, 2018.
Identifiers: LCCN 2017044246 (print) | LCCN 2018001178 (ebook) |
ISBN 9781328694652 (ebook) | ISBN 9781328695277 (hardback) |
ISBN 9781328507990 (paperback)
Subjects: LCSH: Consumer credit—United States. | Finance, Personal—
United States. | BISAC: BUSINESS & ECONOMICS / Personal Finance / General.
Classification: LCC HG3756.U54 (ebook) | LCC HG3756.U54 D38 2018 (print) |
DDC 332.7/43—dc23
LC record available at https://lccn.loc.gov/2017044246

Book design by Chrissy Kurpeski

Printed in the United States of America
DOC 10 9 8 7 6 5 4 3 2 1

*Graphics on pages 17, 88, and 100 are rendered by Houghton
Mifflin Harcourt with data provided courtesy of the author.*

To my wonderful wife, Crystal, and my three boys,
Jackson, William, and Carter;
and to my parents, Lawrence and Cecelia,
who inspire me to be the best man I can be

Contents

·······························

Introduction:
A Cautionary Tale

MY BUSINESS IS SOLVING CREDIT PROBLEMS.

My company in New York City, Regal Credit Management, works with clients of every description — from regular people with nine-to-five jobs to some of the most famous athletes, entertainers, and executives in the world. I sit in my office listening to my clients describe the situations they find themselves in — from bad decisions they've made, to plain old bad luck — and one thread stands out in almost every conversation.

Almost nobody understands how the world of consumer credit really works. It's an industry that touches literally every part of a person's life, from their job, to their home, to their money, but the rules of its game are intentionally kept secret from everyday people. As a result, I hear the same questions over and over again:

- What exactly goes into my credit score?
- How do I build credit when I don't have any, and no banks will talk to me?
- I make good money and pay my bills on time, so why are my credit scores bad?
- How does the bank determine the interest rate I get on a mortgage?
- Why do my credit scores from the bank look different than what I see on credit monitoring services?
- What is a great credit score, and what is a good score?
- What does the perfect credit profile look like?
- How many credit cards should I have, and what is the ideal percentage of my limit to use on credit cards?

Fundamentally, all of these questions come down to a score. The three major credit bureaus, Experian, Equifax, and TransUnion, keep constant tabs on every person in the financial marketplace. If you have a Social Security number and your name is on documentation for a loan, credit card, or mortgage, you're in the system — and the system generates a score for you through a risk-assessment profiling company called FICO.

That score will rank you, and that rank will have a gigantic impact on your life. But the vast majority of people only think about their credit score when they need something — a home loan, student loans, a car loan, a credit card — or when they have a problem. And when they do interact with the world of credit, they do it from a position of weakness. They rely on the "system" to spit out an accurate assessment of their creditworthiness and trust the lender to give them a fair interest rate. But it doesn't work that way!

In reality, your credit reports are filled with arbitrary and often inaccurate information. If you don't know which key items count in the eyes of the credit bureaus, you can't make the best decisions about how to prioritize your financial life. And if you don't know how to check your credit reports for old, inaccurate, or downright fraudulent information, you won't even know why you're being given the interest rate you get on a certain credit card or loan — or why you've been declined.

Even if they do know what their *real* credit score is (which is a totally different thing than the pretend "informational" score the credit bureaus will often show as a part of a credit card promotion), most people have no idea how their creditors and the credit bureaus evaluate that information.

What matters? What doesn't? The credit bureaus want you to believe that it's a complicated story and that they're looking out for you. But it isn't, and they aren't. There *are* rules, and you can use them to make sure you're being given a fair shake. I'm going to show you how.

Credit isn't a new thing. For as long as people have been using money, they have been establishing lines of credit to buy now and then pay later. But our relationship with credit is much different today than it was even thirty years ago. Today, you need a credit score — and, by extension, some debt or the ability to go into debt — just to be able to function in the modern economy. Don't believe me? Just try to rent a car or book a hotel room without a credit card, or apply for a job or rent an apartment or buy some insurance with no credit score.

This credit culture has made consumer debt and the structure necessary to manage it into a huge business. In 2016, Americans collectively carried $750 billion in credit card debt, $1.3 *trillion* in school loan debt, $1 trillion in auto loan debt, and $8.4 trillion in mortgage debt. That's an awful lot of interest being paid, statements being mailed, call centers being staffed, and profit being taken. The largest credit card company in the world, Visa, has 2.5 billion cards in circulation. In 2016, it made $6 billion in profit on 83 billion transactions. America's largest bank, JPMorgan Chase, made $21 billion in profit on $837 billion in loans and employed 234,000 people in 2015.

You don't have to go back too far to find a completely different landscape. In 1970, 51 percent of all Americans reported having a credit card — and a vast majority of those cards were linked to a specific business, like a department store or gasoline company. The average balance? Less than $900. If you wanted a mortgage, you went down to the local bank and sat down with a loan officer, who went through your deposit and job history. The median home price was $23,000, which made the monthly loan payment on an $18,000 loan just about $132 at 8 percent. School loans were virtually nonexistent, and car loans averaged about $100 per month at 11.5 percent interest.

By 2014, 71 percent of all Americans had credit cards, and a vast majority of those cards were bank cards, like a Visa or MasterCard.

Now, the average consumer carries more than $8,000 in revolving debt, and the median home price is up to $223,000. That translates into a monthly mortgage payment of $850 on $178,000 borrowed—to go with the $200 minimum credit card payment, $505 average car loan payment, and $280 average school loan payment every month.

In other words, it's a different world, in more ways than one.

But here's the basic problem: as we spend more and more each month on credit card payments, car payments, and so on, we become more and more dependent on this financial "system" just to function in basic day-to-day life.

That's a problem, because the lenders (and the credit bureaus that compile information and data for them) are *not* on your team. In many cases, what is good for the lender isn't so good for you. Your credit card or mortgage banker is almost always trying to collect as much money in the form of interest and fees as possible while still providing you with the ongoing loan. It's an adversarial relationship, a relationship that is designed to take advantage of you if you don't know the rules. It's as though you walked into a car dealership and dealt with a salesman you didn't know.

But at least at the car dealership, you would probably come in with some basic research about the car you wanted and the price you should pay—and you could then shop around at a few different dealers to find your best deal. In the world of consumer credit, most people don't understand where to look, what to ask, or how to make sure they're getting treated fairly. Unless you learn exactly how credit works, how to manage it, and how to protect it from getting abused, damaged, or stolen, you're essentially closing your eyes and leaving one of the most important pieces of your life to luck and chance. In short, you're taking a big risk.

I'm here to fix that.

I used to be on the other side. After I got out of college, I worked my way up through Bank of America's mortgage lending department to eventually be one of the top loan originators in the country. From there, I went to Wells Fargo and reached that firm's highest performance tier in home mortgage origination. At both banks, I learned exactly how the consumer credit industry works — and how the lenders and the *credit bureaus themselves* are working together to extract as much cash from you as possible. I know exactly how banks and other lenders evaluate borrowers, and I know what kinds of decisions (both good and bad) have the biggest impact on your credit scores.

I built my mortgage business with the intent that I would work on the borrower's side to give them the best deal possible, so that good word of mouth would build my client base. I might not make as much money on each loan, but I'd have an army of happy customers who would come back again and again — and also tell their friends. This approach worked, but as time went on, mortgage lenders across the country gradually got wise to this and made internal rules *prohibiting* their loan originators from offering borrowers key information that might help them save some money.

That left a bad taste in my mouth. And so, since 2010, I've been working full-time on the consumer's side, arming them with better and more accurate information so they can engage lenders and the credit bureaus in a fair fight. In less than ten years, Regal Credit Management has become the largest consumer credit management firm in New York City and has helped thousands of high-profile (and not-so-high-profile) clients navigate the consumer credit landscape.

But I'm not just a guy who used to work at a bank. I've been there personally. I know what it feels like to be almost overcome by the stress and fear — even panic — that can come with dealing with powerful forces like creditors and the credit bureaus.

In 2007, at the beginning of the financial crisis, the mortgage origination business basically vanished, almost overnight. Banks suddenly stopped lending, and the government imposed far more strict documentation standards for every loan. The loan pipeline went empty, and my livelihood disappeared. In the space of six months, I went from a guy cruising along making his own house and car payments and socking away money in the bank to one trying desperately to keep his head above water. Eventually, I declared personal bankruptcy, lost my house to foreclosure, and had to start over again.

As I was picking up the pieces, I realized how much information I had about how credit decisions are made — and how little the average person knows about this subject. It's something that affects virtually every part of our lives, but most people treat their credit scores as some sort of unknowable mystery — mostly because that's how creditors and the credit bureaus *want* it to be perceived.

It probably would have been easy for the game to continue along its merry way if the financial meltdown and Great Recession hadn't hit in late 2007. When the mortgage business tightened and the economy went into a tailspin, lots and lots of people got hurt. Their homes were foreclosed upon, they lost jobs, and they took big financial hits. All of a sudden, millions of people were now *forced* to confront their credit situation. A lot of them discovered just how much they didn't know about the processes that creditors used to evaluate them.

Even though the worst of the economic slowdown has passed, a lot of the same warning signals continue to flash. There still isn't any real transparency from the credit bureaus. People still don't know how that business works — and what the real ramifications of their good and bad decisions are — and folks in literally every income category are getting beat up by the credit market. The proof walks through my office door every day.

Push one of the presets on your car radio and go to your favorite popular music station. If you listen for twenty minutes, you'll probably hear a song by one particular artist whose name you'd recognize immediately. If you went to one of those celebrity net worth sites and plugged in this artist's name, you'd get a number north of $50 million.

You would think that a person with that kind of fame and money wouldn't have any credit issues, right? But that singer is actually one of my clients and had a problem that took several people on my staff almost six months to solve. Identity theft, along with mismanagement by credit bureaus, created such a mess that the artist was in danger of being declined for a mortgage — even with millions of dollars in cash in the bank.

Another one of my clients is a world-famous hip-hop artist who had problems of his own. An inattentive former business manager had ignored a pile of bills and a serious case of identity theft. The performer had also never built up a business credit profile, even though he had a staff of twenty and had earned tens of millions of dollars in royalties and from being on tour. His credit was so bad that he had to personally guarantee a loan for his next tour. Unraveling those issues involved seeking a new Social Security number as well as the meticulous rebuilding of his credit profile over a two-year span.

The average person might not be trying to finance a world concert tour or qualify for an American Express Centurion card, known as the black card. But his or her everyday credit challenges are often strikingly similar.

In *Your Score,* I'm going to show you the step-by-step path to understanding your *real* credit score, how to build the ideal credit profile, and how to protect yourself from predatory lenders, careless mistakes, and even plain bad decisions. I'll take you on a comprehensive tour of a real credit report and show you what all the numbers and notations mean.

You'll find out what to look for in your report and also how to understand the context of the information — so you know what you *really* need to worry about. I'll show you how to identify and fix the five biggest mistakes you're probably making with your credit and give you game plans for navigating some very specific credit situations — from preparing to buy a home, to handling credit card negotiations, to recovering from divorce, foreclosure, and bankruptcy.

Knowledge is power, but it's also protection. The most common threat most of us face in the information age isn't a physical crime. It is identity theft. Anyone who doesn't think it could happen to them isn't living in the real world. I do a series of financial literacy clinics in schools around New York City, and in every one of them, a kid with internet access is able to track down enough personal detail on a celebrity in twenty minutes to be able to open an account in his or her name. I'm going to give you the same top-level strategies I share with my clients to prevent identity theft in the first place and to cut it off if it does happen.

When we're finished, you'll have the knowledge and the confidence to take control of your credit and elevate your score. Let's do it.

YOUR SCORE

1

....

What You Don't Know
Can Hurt You

GETTING READY TO BUY A HOME for the first time is one of the most stressful things you do in your financial lifetime. If you're like most people, you probably don't know much about the process, so you go into it hoping you're getting some good and reliable guidance from your Realtor and from the mortgage person your Realtor swears "will take good care of you."

So you go to the bank and sit across the desk from somebody you've never met before and fill out a form that asks for your Social Security number, job history, bank account information, and annual income. You do what you are told and wait to see if you qualify for a loan.

The mortgage originator punches a few keys, scans the screen, and then announces you qualify for such-and-such a loan, at this interest rate, and you have a down payment requirement.

You walk out of the office feeling a mixture of excitement and fear. You can see the path to your new home, but you probably have no idea what you're signing yourself up for — except for thirty years of payments that are bigger than almost any single check you've ever written.

For most, this is a nerve-racking experience.

And it would be nice to feel that all of the people involved in that transaction are on your side and are working to get you the best deal possible. But the hard truth is that the *entire* consumer credit business — from the bureaus that keep track of your credit history, to the credit card companies, auto lenders, and mortgage originators that are in position to give you money, to the credit counseling services that advertise themselves as the solution to your debt problems — are all lined up with one single goal in mind.

They're there to make money. *Your money.*

Those companies are looking to make a profit on everything from the money you borrow to the information you submit just to get the loan process started. And as for that mortgage originator? Regardless of whether or not you actually apply for a loan there or even get approved, they are sending all of your personal data along to an aggregator that then sells it on to other companies that will then advertise their services to you.

In other words, from the very first time you filled out your first application for a student loan or $500-limit credit card, your financial life has been monitored, inspected, and sliced and diced by hundreds of different companies. They're evaluating you on your performance, predicting your financial future, and figuring out how to sell you more stuff.

But that isn't all. All the data that those companies are compiling gets crunched into a set of three numbers that make up your credit score. That score is being used by insurance companies, potential employers, landlords — even potential spouses — to see where you stand and how you measure up financially.

Most people have no idea who has eyes on their financial life, how things like credit scores are calculated, and specifically what kinds of bad things can happen when they don't pay their bills on time. It's sort of like walking into a casino and playing a table game where there are no rules listed and nobody is there to explain what to do. You're just putting your money down and hoping nobody rips you off too badly.

Even if you're one of the few people who understands a little bit about how the world of consumer credit works and is aware of what credit scores are and how they work, you're still probably not getting the real information that lenders and other companies are using to judge you. Most of the free credit reports you receive online or through a special offer from your credit card company are just weak estimates of your true credit scores — and can be off by as much as 50 points. And 50 points is the difference between qualifying for the best rate you can get on a mortgage or being stuck with a subprime loan that costs you tens of thousands more dollars.

Let's say you're one of the very few who knows the full picture of their financial life, and you're doing a great job keeping track of your credit and protecting yourself and your personal information. In fact, you can have totally perfect data security within your home and your computer, but it just takes one careless merchant that doesn't invest in robust digital security to accidentally leave an open door for a hacker to take your Social Security number, account number, address, and all the other personal information they need to rip you off.

I'm not trying to frighten you, but there's plenty that should make you concerned about what's happening out there without your knowledge. According to the terrific documentary film *Maxed Out: Hard Times, Easy Credit, and the Era of Predatory Lenders* (which you can watch on YouTube here: https://www.youtube.com /watch?v=DsgyybSanCQ), 90 percent of all credit reports provided by U.S. credit bureaus have inaccurate information in them. And the fastest growing problem affecting the security of your credit report isn't a criminal stealing your identity. It's your file being accidentally merged with somebody else's and having your credit scores hurt by information that doesn't have anything to do with you.

You would think that the credit bureaus — organizations whose

4

goal is to collect comprehensive financial information on as many people as possible so that creditors can predict risk — would want to have the right and correct information assigned to the right and correct person. But there's no incentive for them to fix anything, ever. Why? Because in the vast majority of cases, the mistakes on a person's credit report are causing their credit to be judged more negatively, not more positively. And customers with lower credit scores end up getting charged more interest, which can be more profitable for lenders.

It's not just me saying it. In 2011, the three main credit bureaus, Experian, TransUnion, and Equifax, settled a class action lawsuit for $45 million brought by almost a million plaintiffs. In the suit, the consumers charged the credit bureaus with failing to accurately report the discharging of debts and for failing to investigate when consumers disputed a record on their reports. In addition to paying the lawsuit settlement, the bureaus were also required to go back and correct the records of more than one million consumers who had filed for bankruptcy going all the way back to 2003.

In another case, an Oregon woman won an $18.6 million lawsuit against Equifax in 2013 after spending years trying to correct mistakes on her credit report that appeared when her file was merged with one for another person. She was denied by a variety of lenders based on the inaccurate information that she had tried to remove on eight separate occasions over three years.

And in 2015, Equifax settled a lawsuit filed by eight consumers who complained that the credit bureau misrepresented the source of public record information that it was placing on its credit reports. If you read your credit report from Equifax and it showed a tax lien, bankruptcy, or other court-related judgment, Equifax reported the source of that material as the specific court where those judgments occurred. But Equifax wasn't getting that information directly from the courts. It was aggregating it from other sources, like a website that publishes links to stories from other media. The lawsuit claimed that Equifax didn't verify the information to make sure it was up-to-date and free of errors.

Just how powerful is this information vacuum? The Consumer Federation of America did a survey in 2016 that found that 32 percent of American consumers had never accessed their credit report, and another 44 percent hadn't requested a report in the last year. And the reports referred to in that survey were the ones that summarize the last two years of your credit history — not the comprehensive, real reports you need to have to get a complete picture of where you stand.

The time has come to demystify the entire consumer credit business so you can see exactly what kind of information is being tracked, how it's being used, and how you can control it to best serve *your* interests, not just your creditors'. It all starts with your score.

What Is Your Score?

The consumer credit industry is massive, with hundreds of millions of credit accounts active and more being added (and closed) every day. It's way different from how it was fifty years ago, when you walked into your local bank and applied for and received a mortgage from a person you probably knew personally. Now, mega-corporations like Chase and American Express are making almost instantaneous decisions about you and your finances, and they need a way to be able to judge you quickly.

A credit score is an elegant solution. It lets an untrained customer service representative (or a computer) take one quick look at your credit score number and give you a thumbs-up or thumbs-down. These days, companies can process millions of applications and other requests automatically, instead of going through the laborious process of manually underwriting every potential loan.

A credit score also serves an extremely effective secondary

purpose. Since so much of your financial life relies on your credit scores, you're motivated not to damage those scores by failing to pay your bills on time. If you owe American Express $500, Amex is much more likely to get its money because you're afraid of what will happen if you *don't* pay it back. It could sue you for the money and win, but the penalties you will then pay in the form of higher interest and worse terms across all of your other accounts is way, way more painful than just that $500.

That system of scoring is managed by the three credit bureaus (yes, the same ones that have had problems keeping their consumer data straight). Experian, TransUnion, and Equifax are the official clearinghouses for consumer credit data. If you're a lender, you sign up with one of the bureaus (or all of them) to collect information on all your accounts, and the bureaus then aggregate the data from your accounts with accounts from thousands of other creditors.

For example, if you have two credit card accounts, two student loans, a car loan, and a mortgage, the credit bureaus will likely have a complete record of when you originated those accounts, how much you've paid on them, if your payments have been on time, and how close you are to your credit limit on any of the revolving accounts. That's hundreds or even thousands of data points just in your file. And if you've ever used your Social Security number to apply for a loan, you have one of those files.

Once all that data has been aggregated, the bureaus use third-party algorithms to compare your data with millions of other people who have had similar data sets over the years. The algorithms basically estimate how good you're going to be at paying your bills and what kind of risk you'll present to a potential lender. What comes out is an assessment of each person's creditworthiness on a numerical scale.

That is . . . *your score.*

The subscribers to the bureaus can then use those scores as a benchmark for whether or not to offer a potential customer a loan and also to determine on what terms that loan will be issued. If you think of consumer credit as kind of a game, the credit bureaus are the scorekeepers. But it's important to mention again that the scorekeepers are hired by your creditors (the lenders who have given out the money) — *not you* — so they aren't necessarily looking out for your best interests.

Those credit scores get output onto the scale that you're probably at least a little bit familiar with. You're rated on a scale from 300 to 850, with 850 being a "perfect" credit score. You should also know that this score moves up and down based on factors like your payment history, how close you are to your credit limit, and what other kinds of credit accounts you own. Where you stand on that numerical scale lets lenders put you into a certain credit category.

As you'll discover in stories throughout this book, this is a big deal, because a small change in your credit scores can have a massive and cascading impact on what kinds of credit you're able to get and the rates you'll pay for it.

In the next chapter, I'll give you a full rundown on what goes into your credit scores and various ways you can improve those numbers.

What Hurts Your Score and What Doesn't?

I'm sure you already know that missing a payment on your credit card or any other account isn't good for your credit scores. And that being late on your mortgage payments can eventually put you at risk for losing your home to foreclosure. But there are dozens of tight financial situations that many people find themselves in every month, and they make important decisions about what to do based on guesswork and misinformation — and they make these decisions while in total denial or complete panic.

The lack of specific information about what consequences are out there can make *every* situation seem like a four-alarm fire, or it can lull you into thinking something isn't a big deal when it's actually dropping a bomb on your credit score. So when is it time to worry, and when do you have a little more of a grace period? What kinds of items should be getting more attention? In this book, you're going to learn the real story.

As you'll discover, there are plenty of fairy tales, misinformation, and half-truths to wade through to get to the real stuff. For example, one of the biggest misconceptions about a credit score is that it has something to do with your income. It doesn't. You can make $1 million a year and have lousy credit. Likewise, you can be unemployed and have an 800 credit score.

The second biggest misconception is that if you pay all your bills on time, you're automatically going to have excellent credit. Paying on time is great — and as you'll see in the next chapter, it has a strong influence on your scores — but it isn't the only factor. At least 65 percent of your score has nothing to do with your promptness at sending a check or paying online. You're measured by how much debt you carry in relation to your credit lines, your payment history, the kinds of credit accounts you have, and how much credit you've been applying for recently.

When it comes to damaging your scores, it works a lot like tearing down a building. Some knocks on the outside walls produce superficial damage, while kicking out the foundation will make the building collapse a lot faster. Making a few payments a day or two late likely won't have any impact on your credit scores, because most creditors don't report those kinds of misses to the bureaus. But if you start missing mortgage payments — which in the hierarchy of credit accounts are considered the most important — you can trash your credit score by up to 100 points in less than 60 days.

We're going to talk a lot more about the various kinds of credit accounts in the chapters to come, but here I want to give you a brief and straightforward list that covers what the most damaging acts to your credit scores are. I do this both to focus your attention on those things you don't want to be doing and also to give you a frame of reference for the relative amount of damage certain mistakes can cause.

1. MISSING A MORTGAGE PAYMENT

As I said, mortgage payments count the most in the hierarchy, and missing even one is hard on your score. These payments also tend to be the biggest ones you're making, which can make catching up on them very difficult. Once you're 90 days past due on a payment, the loan holder can start the foreclosure process.

2. GOING DELINQUENT ON A STUDENT LOAN

Most student loans are backed by the federal government, which means the debt can't be discharged in bankruptcy. And if you're delinquent on a student loan, the collection agency can go after your paycheck through a garnishment and even take your federal income tax refund. The good news is that school loans aren't usually reported as delinquent for 60 days, which gives you a short grace period to get current.

3. GOING 60 DAYS LATE ON A CAR PAYMENT

Missing a car payment is high in the hierarchy of "bad things" for your credit score both because of the value the credit algorithms put on this kind of installment loan and because of the practical consequences of losing your car. At 60 days, car lenders can start the repossession process.

4. IGNORING A TAX DEBT

Tax debts are like student loans in that they can't be discharged through bankruptcy. They'll also follow you around and make it hard for you to conduct any other official transactions with the government entity to which you owe the debt.

5. GOING INTO DEBT COLLECTIONS ON A CREDIT CARD

Credit card companies generally start charging off your debt (that is, writing it off as permanently delinquent) and moving it to a collection agency after 180 days. This presents several big problems, not including the big hit to your credit score. Once the account has been charged off, your credit card is closed, so you can't use it anymore. You also still owe the debt, along with a stack of fees added on by the collection agency. By the way, credit card companies can hit you with a late fee and a penalty interest rate even if you're *one* day late on a payment. But the lasting pain comes from a hit to your credit score. That starts happening at the 30-day mark.

6. GOING 90 DAYS LATE ON A MEDICAL DEBT

Medical debts carry less weight in the algorithm than other kinds of debt, but a collection is a collection. At 90 days, these debts often get sold to collection agencies — and even that is in the process of changing. Because of the nature of medical debt, the New York State attorney general is moving to demand that the bureaus not report medical collections for at least 180 days.

7. MAXING OUT A CREDIT CARD

Your debt-to-credit-line ratio is a big part of how your credit score is determined. If you run your cards up to the limit, this ratio will obviously not be good.

Being late by a day or two on a payment generally doesn't hurt your credit scores — although it may subject you to late fees and a penalty interest rate by your credit card company.

Also, people often wonder whether a change in their job status has anything to do with their score. If you lose your job or start making much less income, that won't be reflected in your overall credit score. Of course, some loans require income verification in addition to a credit score, and those would obviously be affected.

The way credit inquiries — creditors accessing your credit report to see if you qualify for a loan — affect your credit score is often misunderstood. You do take a small hit to your score every time a potential lender does what's called a "hard inquiry," meaning a check of your credit because you've applied for a new account. The hit is designed to warn the system of somebody who is trying to add to their debt burden — and the penalty becomes larger the more hard inquiries that come in during a short period of time. But one inquiry has a very small effect, and that hit disappears within a few months.

How Else Is Your Score Being Used?

So here's a common question: If you're not planning to buy a house and your credit card debt doesn't seem like that big of a deal, why should you be concerned about your credit score? The reality is that your scores are being used for way more than just strictly financial purposes.

Since at least the mid-1990s, insurance companies have used credit scores as part of their policy-underwriting process for both car and life insurance. A large study released by the Federal Trade Commission (FTC) in 2007 conclusively established a link between credit scores and auto accident claims — which means that people with lower credit scores tend to file more and also have more expensive car insurance claims. Auto insurers use this information along with driving records to put customers into risk pools. Bottom line? If your credit scores are lousy, you're going to pay more for car insurance.

This connection isn't as strong with life insurance, but if you've declared bankruptcy within the last year, it's pretty certain that no insurance company will issue you a policy. And if you note specific financial issues on your life insurance application, the life insurance company *will* ask to run a credit check.

Two other arenas where credit scores are used extensively are in the employment world and in the rental market. A credit check is routinely required for a variety of jobs related to financial services, and many employers from all sorts of different industries do credit checks of potential employees who are finalists for a job. The Society for Human Resource Management did a study that revealed six out of ten employers in the private sector do some form of credit history check during the hiring process.

You should know that potential employers do have to notify you if they're going to perform a credit check — and they need to use your Social Security number to run the check. The credit reports that employers see are different and less detailed than the ones creditors see as well. For example, they don't include credit scores or information identifying specific accounts, just information pertaining to delinquencies, bankruptcies, and legal judgments.

If you're in the market for a rental home, most landlords are going to require a credit check before they let you move in. They basically want to get a look at your payment history to see if you have a record of walking away from your debts. Your credit report contains public records relating to any bankruptcies, foreclosures, and evictions you might have had — all the kinds of factors landlords take into consideration.

How Do You Find Out What Your Credit Score Is?

This is important: if you based your knowledge of the credit landscape just on the advertisements you saw on television and received through email solicitation, you'd probably think that the reports you can get from FreeCreditReport.com would be more than sufficient to verify a lot of the information we're going to talk about in this book.

You would be wrong.

Those free reports are what are called "consumer education reports," which are not compiled using the same algorithms and data as real credit reports. I'm not saying those reports are worthless. They can be a decent starting point for your investigation.

But the free reports you get online generally only cover two years of transactions, and in addition, they don't necessarily show your activity with all of your creditors. The score on one of those reports can vary dramatically from what your real scores show. I've had clients show me results of a free credit report that had them listed at 760 — a very good score — only to then get the real scores and find them in the high 600s. That can make for the difference between qualifying for the best mortgage program at your bank and getting declined for a loan!

The very best credit report is called a "tri-merge," and it can only be ordered by a mortgage or banking professional. It pulls together the reports from all three bureaus and combines duplicate information. I've found that the best way to get one of these reports is to make friends with your Realtor or mortgage originator at the local branch of your bank. Your Realtor will have good relationships with originators and bankers who want him or her to send business, so they'll be willing to run a report for you.

But if you can't get access to that kind of report, the next best kind comes from MyFICO.com. FICO is the company that creates the algorithms that actually crunch all the data that the credit bureaus collect. For about $60, you can get FICO's version of a tri-merge, which will give you estimated scores from all three credit bureaus, along with a score simulator that will show you what could happen to your credit score if you make certain changes to the mixture and balances on your current accounts. The only difference between the MyFICO report and the real, professional version of your credit report is that the professional version covers a longer time frame. I've found the scores from the MyFICO report to be the closest to the real ones out of any of the nonprofessional choices.

Just to sum up: You can go into the credit process without any of the information we're going to talk about in this book, but you'll be at the mercy of somebody else's profit motive. One of my clients came to me because she was in the process of applying for a mortgage loan through a bank that she had used for more than ten years. Her mortgage originator said he was very familiar with her credit profile, and he thought he could get her a great rate on a loan.

Based upon those assurances, she didn't take any extra steps beyond filling out the mortgage application, and she was disappointed when she was prequalified for a loan that was for less than she was hoping. She then went outside her bank to shop around and see if she could secure a larger prequalification letter. The very first stop she made at a different bank was, well, an eye-opener. It turned out that her credit score was terrific, and she could easily qualify for a much better product than the one her original banker was trying to sell her. (My guess is that the original loan offer was probably one that the first bank was offering incentives to its originators in order to push it through to clients.)

The difference between the two loans? More than $450 per month in payments. My client took the second loan offer and was able to pay for her property taxes, too — just with the extra amount she saved by shopping around a bit and getting a look at her real credit scores.

Let the buyer beware.

2

....

What's in Your Score?

NOW THAT YOU KNOW what the game is and what the stakes are, it's time to decipher the scoreboard.

You've read about how the three credit bureaus compile information about your history and sell that data to creditors so they can make decisions about lending you money. And now you know why so many of the "free credit reports" you can get are worth about what you paid for them.

In this chapter, I'm going to take you on a comprehensive tour of your *real* score. I'll show you how the bureaus are truly measuring you, what things you do that help and hurt your scores, and how to make sure there's no information on your credit reports that doesn't belong there.

It all starts with FICO. Originally known as Fair, Isaac and Company, FICO started in 1956 as a service to help lenders make faster, more accurate loan decisions.

The methods FICO uses today are way more sophisticated than those of the 1950s, but the overall concept is still the same. The company figures out what factors make people more or less likely to default on a loan, and it builds formulas called algorithms to make those predictions.

FICO sells those algorithms to the credit bureaus, which then use the data they collect on your payment history, balances, and other borrower information to come up with your credit score.

Here's where it gets confusing. Each credit bureau collects data in subtly different ways. For example, they might collect data at different times or collect it more or less frequently. So when each bureau plugs its own set of data into the FICO algorithms, it comes up with a different score.

That means you might have a 700 credit score with Equifax, but a 720 with Experian and TransUnion. This is important to know because various lenders use different credit bureaus to check your score. So if you have a great score with one but a lesser one with the other two, the higher score isn't going to help you if it's with a credit bureau that your lender isn't using. And since lenders have to pay to have their data recorded by the bureaus, some smaller companies might report to only one or two of them, while the big credit card companies and department stores will report to all three. The system is designed both to give creditors a way to quickly judge risk and incentivize borrowers not to flake out on their debts because the "debt police" are watching.

Another complication comes from the algorithm that FICO produces. FICO actually sells a variety of algorithms to lenders, each of them designed to weigh risk for a particular kind of borrower. There's a "universal" FICO algorithm, but there's also one specifically designed for car loans and another for credit cards.

FICO's algorithms are secret, but we do know the relative importance of some factors — or, the basic ingredients of the credit pie:

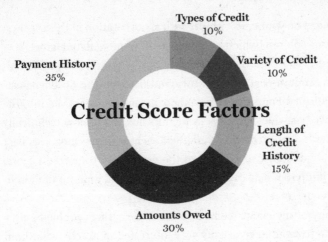

Types of Credit
10%

Payment History
35%

Variety of Credit
10%

Credit Score Factors

Length of
Credit
History
15%

Amounts Owed
30%

Payment History

Whether or not you pay your bills on time is obviously a big concern to a potential lender, so it's probably not a surprise that payment history is given the greatest weight in your credit score. One of the first questions I always get from a new client is about the relative pain of a late or missed payment. How late does it have to be before it really hurts you, and what is the relative damage a missed payment causes?

Like most answers, it all depends.

Technically, any loan payment that is more than 30 days late can be reported to the credit bureaus for delinquency. But for practical purposes, that almost never happens. Companies usually report all of their data to the bureaus on the same day every month, and your payment is unlikely to be due on or around that date. Many, many companies don't even report monthly, so being just shy of 30 days late with a payment — and getting it in before the next payment request is mailed — is not going to do any damage.

But it's safe to say that if you actually *miss* two payments, you'll be dinged on your credit report with an annotation in the 30-days-past-due column (which we'll talk about in more detail later).

And if you miss three payments, you're going to be taken out of the 30-days-past-due category and listed in the 60-days-past-due category. Four missed payments means you've moved into the 90-days-past-due category — which means you're now technically in default. Even worse, the effect of each of those categories isn't a simple doubling or tripling of the damage to your credit score. Each jump to a new category is an exponential amount of pain to your credit score.

Many of my clients come in with some serious problems they need to fix, so they're usually very interested in exactly what kind of damage a 90-day or delinquent account can do to their scores. That also depends. If you come in with great credit and all of a sudden have a delinquency, your score will get pounded — often by more than 100 points. That's because the delinquency is reporting a change of your circumstance. You used to be a great risk, but now you're showing a lot more reason to worry. If you have bad credit, however, that delinquency is pretty much already priced into your score. It'll hurt you, but probably to the tune of around 20 points.

It's important to mention that all of these penalties are specific to your *credit score*, not your standing with your lender. For example, many credit card companies will hit you with a penalty interest rate if you miss a payment — even if they don't report you as delinquent to the credit bureaus. Your credit score stays the same, but you're paying way more in interest because you made a mistake.

There's nothing to the old myth that you have to carry balances on your cards in order to improve your score (see below), but one thing you *do* have to do to prove a good payment history on a particular account is to actually use the account. In other words, if you have a credit card and don't ever charge anything on it, the account will show up as inactive on your credit report, and you won't get the benefit of a great payment history. Now, you don't have to do anything crazy — just make some small purchases each month with each of your cards and pay them off in full at the end of the cycle.

I'm also generally not in favor of keeping debt when you can get rid of it, but under certain circumstances, it's good to be able to show a long history of prompt payments — especially if you're getting ready to apply for a mortgage or a car loan. Paying off a small home equity line will rob you of that payment history and hurt your score. It's OK to hold on to the debt in the short term until you're set with your big-ticket credit maneuvers, and then pay it off when you anticipate having a quiet period.

One last thing to remember about making your payments is that the amount you owe doesn't really matter if the debt goes into delinquency or default. Let me explain: defaulting on a $100 medical debt hurts just as much as defaulting on $10,000 worth of credit card debt. The extra credit card debt obviously hurts you more when it comes to your utilization percentage (which we'll talk about in a minute), but the whack your score takes from the late payments is the same, no matter the amount. And since your payment history makes up the biggest percentage of your score, that's a very important factor to keep in mind.

Amounts Owed

This category is one that might seem simple but is actually often misunderstood. It stands to reason that if you owe a lot of money, you're going to be considered more of a credit risk than somebody who owes less money. But, curiously, that's not exactly true.

What credit card companies care more about is your "utilization rate," or the percent of your available credit you're actually carrying from month to month. For example, if you have three credit cards with a total limit of $10,000 and you carried a balance of $1,000 forward, your utilization rate would be 10 percent.

Why does this matter? Because you might owe the same $1,000

as the next two people in line with you at Starbucks, but if the first person has $1,000 in available credit and the second person has $100,000, all of your situations are very different.

If you have very large credit limits and no debt on your credit cards, you'll be seen favorably for your low utilization rate, but you could raise some red flags for how deeply into the hole you could find yourself in not much time. In other words, if you're carrying three cards with a total limit of $50,000 and you have a zero balance on any of those three, lenders might consider how much total debt you already have access to before giving you access to more. Now, just to be clear: I'm not suggesting you'd have a *bad* credit score under that scenario, but adding more *potential* debt just because you qualify for it isn't always the right or best strategy.

I don't have a specific rule of thumb for my clients about what kind of income they should have in relation to the credit lines they carry, but I do use one measuring stick. For each card, you should have a personal firm limit that you would use no more than 25 percent unless you were in an emergency. That is, if you have a $10,000-limit card, you should be thinking about carrying no more than $2,500 on it month to month. If you carry more, you should be thinking about getting another card to distribute that balance over two cards, which we'll discuss in Chapter 7.

If you do carry balances on your cards, bear in mind that you will start to negatively affect your score once you carry over the first dollar of balance. That means you shouldn't be carrying a balance near your credit limit on one low-limit card while carrying small balances on other credit cards. For example, if you have three cards with a total of $20,000 in credit allocated at a $2,000 limit for one card, $10,000 for another, and $8,000 for a third, you will get hit with up to a 50-point penalty if you carry $2,000 on the $2,000-limit card and zero on the other two instead of distributing your debt *proportionally* across the cards. That's because the creditor who has given you the low-limit card isn't concerned about any of your other cards. It's only interested in getting paid on *its* debt, and if you're maxed out on that card, you will show up as a risk. You'll get a good "grade" from the two other creditors but will take a hit from the low-limit one.

Creditors don't know what your income is, so they have no way of knowing if a high utilization rate is a problem for you or not. Extremely wealthy clients often come to me looking for answers about their low credit scores, and after some digging, we usually find that they have a random low-limit credit card like a Macy's or Mobil that has a high balance on it. The high utilization rate on that one card may be enough to cost them a credit score in the top tier, which is a painful situation when you're looking to secure a multimillion-dollar loan.

If you're getting ready to make a big-ticket purchase, like a home or a car, you need to be even more strict about your credit utilization. Zero balances are best, but staying under 10 percent in the 90 days leading up to closing on those loans is generally going to let the lenders see you as "safe."

Length of Credit History

You can think of your length of credit history as your letter of reference. If you've had a long relationship with a bank through a mortgage or with a credit card company though your card, it shows you have been a stable, responsible customer. That's valuable for a creditor to see.

Of course, everybody has to start somewhere, which is why it's important to get in the game as soon as possible — even with a low-limit secured card backed by the funds in a checking account. The more that account ages over time, the better it looks on your credit report.

What exactly is the overall impact of the length of your credit history? Accounts that are under six months old have virtually *no* positive impact on your scores and can actually hurt them if you've already missed payments or have charged up the balances. Once you've had an account open for a year, you will start to see a 30- or 40-point gradual trickle of improvement to your scores. By the time an account has remained in good standing for seven years — the full time a legitimate credit report measures — you're getting the total benefit of that history.

Many of my clients come to me with what they think is a solid plan for getting out of financial trouble, and it involves paying off and closing their credit cards. Now, reducing debt is great, but closing accounts that you've had for a long time is almost never a successful strategy. Even if you don't use that department store card you've had since college, the positive payment history you have on it for all those years (assuming, of course, that you *do* have a good payment history) is worth its weight in gold. Cancelling after zeroing out the balance will actually hurt you more than paying off the balance helped you. Remember, shutting down a credit card on which you have had a long and consistent financial history of paying your bills is not necessarily a good idea.

As a result, the best strategy is to protect your longest-lived accounts with good payment history and make them the backbone of your credit mix. If you do need to add a variety of credit lines (which we're about to discuss), be selective about where you add and subtract.

Variety of Credit

Evaluating your credit mix is a lot like evaluating a prospect for the NBA draft. If a player can shoot really well but doesn't have any other skills, he is seen as a one-dimensional player and graded accordingly. Similarly, if you have a bunch of credit card accounts but no mortgage, car loans, school loans, or other kinds of installment debt, the FICO algorithm will see you as equally one-dimensional and ding you accordingly.

We'll talk more about building the best mix of credit lines in the next chapter, but in general, you should have five to seven open lines of credit, and those lines should include at least one example of a revolving account (credit card), installment account (car or student loan), and, ideally, a mortgage. If you're a young person just getting into the game or you're saving for your first house, you're obviously not going to be able to show a mortgage loan. In that case, it's crucial to have some other accounts with at least five years of age and a clean payment history.

New Credit

The essence of a credit score is trying to predict the future by measuring your past behavior. Creditors want to be able to assign a risk factor to you and charge interest accordingly. For them, the goal is to charge you the most interest you'd be willing to pay — and enough to account for the risk that you might walk away from your debt. The credit card companies and mortgage originators absolutely hate it when they have to chase you for the money, because it's expensive and time consuming to do it.

To keep that from happening, the FICO algorithm considers how many new credit lines you've been opening recently. In basic terms, it calculates the average age of your accounts. If you open a bunch of credit lines at once, you will dramatically lower your average account age, especially if you don't have an extensive credit history established.

Your score can also be affected by inquiries into your credit, even if you don't ultimately open the credit line. Most people worry about that when they begin to shop for a mortgage, because they could have a half-dozen mortgage originators pulling their credit report over the course of a few weeks. But the system is built to understand this reality, and it counts any number of mortgage (and car loan and student loan) inquiries made within the same 45 days as a single inquiry.

The "new credit" period is two years, but the impact of any inquiries fades proportionally over that time. A single inquiry probably won't affect your score at all, and a second one will only ding you a few points. And any inquiries you do have will only show up on your credit report for 90 days. We'll talk more about inquiries and new credit accounts in Chapter 3.

How Do I Read This Thing?

If you followed the process in the first chapter, you should already have your tri-merge credit report, which pulls together your credit reports from all three bureaus and (hopefully) removes all duplicate information. The real reports that lenders use come through the bank and show seven years of credit history. If you can't get your hands on one of those, you can order a tri-merge report from MyFICO.com that will give you a reasonable facsimile of your real credit scores — with the major limitation that it only covers the last two years instead of the seven covered by the professional-level report. (You can also flip to the Appendix at the back of this book to see a generic sample credit report.)

The format of the report you're holding might vary slightly, but every tri-merge report is made up of the same basic building blocks:

The Scores
Identification
Summary
Payment History
Credit Score Information

Credit History

Inquiries

Public Records (such as tax liens, judgments, and bankruptcies) usually have their own section beyond the summary
portion

Fraud Alert

The Scores

At the very top of the report are the pieces of information that
most people are looking for: the actual credit scores from each of
the three bureaus. Since the three bureaus collect different information, they will each most likely show a different score, ranging
somewhere between 300 and 850.

When you see your scores, your first reaction is probably going to be to try and figure out where you stand. Are your numbers
good, average, or bad?

According to Experian's numbers, the average American credit
score is just under 700. That falls in the upper half of the "prime"
credit range between 660 and 720, where more than half of consumers fit in. About 20 percent of consumers have credit scores
of 800 or better, while about 15 percent have no credit score at all
because they've never had an account on record with one of the
bureaus.

Whether your credit scores are considered good, bad, or average
depends very much on the context in which they're being judged.
If you're trying to get an American Express black card, a 740 score
may not be good enough. But if you're a first-time homebuyer with
a good down payment, a 740 will get you into the top tier of mortgage programs.

In general, you can break the tiers down according to rough
score categories. If your score is 740 or above, you'll generally

qualify for the best programs and the best interest rates. Scores from 700 to 739 are considered what I would call "A-minus," while scores from 660 to 699 are "average." If you drop below 660, you're in subprime territory, and credit scores below 620 make you essentially a non-factor in the credit markets.

The underwriting guidelines for the lender you're trying to work with are obviously the biggest factor in what kind of interest rate, credit line, or loan terms you're going to get. And it's *extremely* important to understand that lenders use any or all three of the credit bureaus to make their decision. You might have a 760 score with Experian, a 750 with TransUnion, and a 740 with Equifax, but that 760 doesn't do you any good if your credit card company uses one of the other bureaus for your score. In its eyes, it's as if that 760 doesn't exist.

However, when you go to buy a home, your mortgage originator will look at all three scores and use the one in the middle. In most cases, the spread between the highest score and the lowest is around 15 or 20 points, but I've seen cases in which one score was 150 points different than the others. When that happens, you need to do some digging, because it usually means some kind of fraud or mistake is reported on one of the reports.

Identification

In this section, you can see all the names and addresses each bureau has on file for you. By law, the only information that *has* to be here is your name, marital status, and current address. Since identity theft and plain old clerical mistakes cause headaches for a huge number of consumers every single day, be sure to thoroughly vet this information to make sure somebody else hasn't added a false address for you — where they could be diverting statements in order to keep you in the dark about the fact that they've stolen your life — or that your name hasn't simply been mixed up with another similar one. You can write to each bureau and request that any non-current addresses be removed from your file.

One common mistake? I'll often see clients' tri-merge reports with three different names showing up for the same Social Security number. For example, a person named Sandra Jane Smith might have a listing for Sandy Smith, Sandra J. Smith, S. J. Smith, and Sandee Smith — all either variations of her name, misspellings, or attempts by somebody else to establish a credit line by dishonest means.

All kinds of other issues come up when similar addresses, similar names, or mistyped Social Security numbers come into play. I've seen hundreds of examples where the credit reports of two separate people with a similar identifying characteristic were merged into one report. It's a mess and something you want to identify right away and resolve. (We'll talk about the specific methods for fixing those problems in Chapter 4.) One of my clients has been dealing with a mismerged file for years because there is somebody else with the same first and last name who was born in the same state on the same day. Their Social Security numbers are one digit apart. Unfortunately, that other person has had a tough financial life, which means that my client — a successful entrepreneur — has had to monitor her credit religiously to keep the two files from continuing to mix.

You might also notice that your current or previous employers are listed in the information section. This comes from when you're asked to provide your current and previous employers on a credit application. The employer listing has nothing to do with whether or not you're approved for a line of credit. It's there to provide extra information in case a creditor wants to verify that the person it's talking to about an account is the real account holder.

As I said, your best practice should be to make sure that the only information appearing in this box for each credit bureau is your current address. When you write to request that the others be removed, send a basic note that states you don't live at the listed address (or work at a given company) and send with it proof of your Social Security number and copies of two recent bills that show your correct address.

Summary

Near the top of the report is a box that shows your credit score for each of the bureaus, along with the current status and payment summary for the three different kinds of accounts the bureaus measure — real estate loans, installment accounts, and revolving accounts. Across the top of the grid, you'll see categories that are pretty self-explanatory: account type, current balance, minimum payment, number of open accounts, closed accounts, derogatory or negative accounts, past due amount, and the number of times an account has been reported 30, 60, or 90+ days past due.

Across the bottom, you can see a snapshot of all those categories added together. You'll be able to see the total amount you have in loan balances, the minimum payment total for those loans, the total number of accounts, and the total number of times an account has been reported delinquent for the various time frames.

Also included in the summary is the number of "public records" and collection accounts associated with your Social Security number. If you have a bankruptcy, foreclosure, tax lien, or other legal judgment against you that has a financial component, that's noted as a public record. If you have an account that has been moved into collections, that's going to be counted there as well. Both will show up later in your credit history in more detail.

This information is good for getting a snapshot of your overall credit position, but you're going to want to take a deeper dive into the detailed information in the payment history and credit history sections.

Payment History

The credit bureaus are basically relentless data gatherers. They collect information from millions of creditors and aggregate it according to each individual consumer. Your payment history shows the nuts and bolts of this data collection. It breaks out your individual credit accounts by month over the life of the account (or seven years, whichever is longer), and it shows if the account was current or delinquent in a particular month. It's a quick way to see trends in a consumer's financial position. For example, if you had a rough patch five years ago because of job loss and there are a cluster of late payments showing in that time, that's a different view than showing one or two assorted, random late payments in the five years since.

FICO's algorithms place you into certain "scorecards" or templates based on your various credit behaviors. When your late payments happen (and how often they happen) will move you from one risk scorecard to another. Since more recent late payments are seen as more predictive of what you're going to do in the near future, they hurt your score more and move you into a worse scorecard.

In each individual monthly box, the account is also annotated with a color code or symbol to show the escalating seriousness of any delinquency, from 30 to 59 days past due all the way to being passed to collections.

This is the section to which you want to pay close attention if you're trying to negotiate with creditors over a disputed or delinquent account. By checking for errors in how your payments were credited, you have some ammunition in that conversation. Creditors will also sometimes agree to delete negative late payment information for a settlement of the account.

30

Credit Score Information

All of the factors we've been talking about go into the mathematical stew that makes up your credit score from each bureau. In the credit information section, your scores from each one are shown, along with the "reason codes" that represent the main reasons why your score wasn't higher. These are useful to note because resolving them can often be the quickest way to make your scores better.

FICO has an extensive list of codes — 99, to be exact — and they range from 01 (amount owed on accounts is too high) to 99 (lack of recent consumer finance company account information). Some of the more common codes relate to the subjects we've been talking about in this chapter:

07: Account payment history is too new to rate
09: Too many accounts recently opened
11: Amount owed on revolving accounts is too high
18: Number of accounts with delinquency
33: Proportion of loan balances to loan amounts is too high
40: Derogatory public record or collection filed
85: Too few active accounts

For a complete list of FICO reason codes, go to my website, www.anthonymdavenport.com/yourscore. In theory, the codes are supposed to be listed in order of how much they're affecting your score. I haven't found that to be exactly true with my clients. They're useful as a guideline, but they really shouldn't be used as a substitute for the good practices you're going to learn in this book. And if you need more evidence that they aren't foolproof, even clients with

perfect 850 credit (yes . . . they do exist!) will often show four reason codes on their report as to why they don't have an impossible-
to-get 851 score.

Credit History

If your credit summary and payment history are the overview of
your credit score, your *credit history* is the blow-by-blow detail.
Every credit account tracked by each of the bureaus is listed here
with comprehensive information throughout.

It lists:

- The name of the creditor
- The type of credit account
- The account number
- When you opened the account
- If the account is still active and the closing date if it was closed
- Balance
- Credit limit
- Terms of the loan (months remaining)
- Whether the loan is in good standing
- Amount past due
- Any delinquencies and their length
- Which credit bureau is reporting
- The date when the credit bureau last reported data from that
  creditor

Any accounts that have a delinquency or are otherwise reporting something negative are helpfully bolded, which makes them
easy for you to find. But don't stop with just a cursory look. It's useful to go through each account and make sure it's one you recognize. If you closed an account but it's still listed as active, make a

note. If there's a balance that doesn't look familiar, run that question by your lender to verify, and go back to the credit bureaus if you think any of the information is wrong or outdated.

This section is an extremely valuable tool to use at the start of the process of getting control of your credit because it gives you the full landscape of how you're viewed within the world of consumer credit. It's really the only way to verify for yourself if everything in your file is legitimate and there's been no instance of identity theft or other kinds of fraud.

We're going to talk more about that in Chapter 8, where I give a complete rundown on identity theft, but I'll mention one fact here that should inspire you to focus your attention on reviewing your reports carefully. In most cases, the first time a consumer realizes they've been victimized is when they receive a notification from a lender, or on a credit report, that their credit has already been damaged. By checking your scores and their sources carefully, you can be proactive and catch these issues earlier.

Inquiries

Every time you actively request a new line of credit, your request is shown on your credit report as an inquiry. This "hard" inquiry represents the time the creditor went to the credit bureau to pull information about you so it could make a decision. A single act of requesting credit has no negative impact on your score, but if you stack up a variety of unrelated inquiries over the course of a few weeks, you're showing your creditors that you might be significantly increasing your potential debt load, and you will see a resulting drop in your score.

Creditors you already have a relationship with — like your bank or credit card company — can also proactively check your credit to see if you're available for a certain promotional offer or a different interest rate on your loan. These inquiries are called "soft," and they don't have an impact on your score.

All inquiries, hard and soft, are listed in this section, and reviewing the list is another good security practice. If you see hard inquiries that you didn't authorize or that you don't recognize, it's an indicator that somebody has at least some of your personal information and is trying to open a new line of credit in your name. Soft inquiries show which of your creditors are sniffing around — either because you're doing well and they want to sell you more stuff or because you might be having some trouble making payments and they're checking on the status of their loan.

Creditors can and do use your up-to-date score to change the terms of your loan. It's far more common with credit card companies than with any other lenders. If they see your utilization percentage going up and notice you carrying more debt, they'll often lower your credit limit or increase your interest rate because they now judge you to be an increased risk. I'll cover this subject in more detail in Chapter 7, when we talk more about credit cards.

There are a variety of ways to control the way in which inquiries hit your score, and we'll talk more about them in Chapter 8, which covers identity theft.

Fraud Alerts

Federal law under the Fair Credit Reporting Act mandates that the credit bureaus give you a mechanism to require potential creditors to verify that you're the one who is actually applying for the line of credit. That mechanism comes in the form of a fraud alert.

You can sign up for three kinds of fraud alerts. If you suspect that you might be the victim of identity theft, you can sign up for the initial form of fraud alert, which lasts 90 days. It requires lenders to see proof of identity before opening a line of credit in your name.

If you're a confirmed victim of identity theft, you can sign up for an extended fraud alert, which lasts seven years. This alert gives you access to two free credit reports from each bureau in the first twelve months, and you're automatically blocked from soft credit inquiries — even from places where you've been prescreened as an existing customer.

The third type of fraud alert is for members of the military who want more protection while they're out on active duty. It lasts a year, and it also requires creditors to verify your identity and to stop making soft inquiries about your scores.

Your credit reports will summarize which (if any) of these protections you currently have in place. If identity theft has happened to you, these are great first steps to take. You can find the full prescription in Chapter 8.

*

What's not on your credit report? Well, you shouldn't see anything related to your age, race, nationality, or religion. Your current employer could be listed, but there should be no information about your salary or work history.

Interestingly (so to speak), none of the interest rates on your accounts will be listed on your report. You also won't see information on judgments for child or spousal support — unless you default on those obligations and they begin to be enforced through collections.

3
....

Building the Perfect Credit Profile

IT SHOULD BE ABSOLUTELY CLEAR by now that your credit data is getting sliced and diced to an infinite degree by every creditor (or potential creditor). They're judging you and using big data to predict how you're going to handle your financial life over the next two years.

That's a given. If you're going to be categorized by the consumer credit industry — and that characterization is going to dictate so much about how you live your life — you need to understand how you're going to be evaluated. With that information, you can then build a rational, realistic strategy for putting yourself in the most favorable classification you can.

You have something to shoot for.

If your credit scores are your financial fingerprints, your overall credit profile is your entire body of work. Your scores are a snapshot of your financial life. Your profile is the set of choices you make to get those scores, and it's the combination of the financial and personal benchmarks you're meeting.

When you go to apply for a mortgage, your prospective mortgage originator is certainly going to pull your credit scores to take a look at your creditworthiness. But they are also going to ask you a variety of other questions — and will also check a variety of other sources — to obtain a more expansive view of your *credit profile*. Your scores count, but so does your profile.

Your scores show how well you've been able to pay your bills and manage your financial life in the past and predict how well you'll be able to continue to do so in the years to come. Your profile lets lenders put you in a box with millions of other consumers with similar financial characteristics. There, they can see how well those other folks handled their financial responsibilities — and how profitable it was for the lender to do business with them.

What makes up your credit profile? It's a combination of factors. Some are very straightforward, such as your income, stability of employment, stability of residence, liquid assets, and age. Your income and liquid assets give an indication of how easy or hard it would be for you to pay off a loan. When you're getting a mortgage, more liquid assets (and more of a down payment) mean you have more skin in the game, and you'll be less likely to walk away from your payments. Lenders like that because it reduces their risk. Job stability and housing stability show that you're able to build productive and long-term relationships — which is exactly what a creditor like a mortgage originator is looking for. Your age can have either a sliding benefit or demerit. The reality for most fifty-five-year-olds is that they don't have twenty more years in the job market. So, if you are fifty-five and signing up for a longer-term mortgage, that's a factor the lender is going to take into consideration. If you're twenty-four and you don't have much credit history, even a high income isn't enough to overcome this lack of track record.

Other factors are less transparent. Like your credit score itself, your credit profile is influenced by the kinds of debt you hold. You're rewarded for having a variety of debt "flavors" — installment loans, revolving debt, mortgage debt — because it shows a lender you're able to manage different kinds of expenses on a steady month-to-month basis. It also provides more data points for the lenders' algorithms to measure you by, and more data means a more accurate assessment of risk.

Thinking about your financial decisions in terms of how they will affect your credit scores is fine in the short term, but to have long-term success, you want to transition that thinking into considering what your credit profile is and what you want it to be. With a strong credit profile (and good credit scores!), you'll have the ultimate freedom in your financial life — and that's the freedom of choice. When you can make decisions on your own time and with the right information, you're in a much better position than the person who is finding that they are being forced into a particular course of action out of fear, frustration, or a simple lack of better alternatives.

To illustrate the relationship between credit scores and credit profiles, it's useful to look at a big study Credit Karma did of more than 200,000 of its customers. Instead of compiling a simple tally of those 200,000 consumers' scores and breaking it down by percentages, Credit Karma drilled down to find out what specific financial traits the customers in the various credit score brackets actually had.

At the end of the survey, it was able to develop a composite model of what somebody with a credit score of 800 or above looks like financially, along with people from 700 to 799, 600 to 699, 500 to 599, and below 500.

The point of all that data isn't to compare yourself to what other people are doing (although it's hard to resist). The best use of the information is to see some important pieces of the credit profile of somebody who is truly winning the credit game. It's a way to reverse engineer what kinds of accounts and behaviors people with a good credit score have and then add in those other pieces of the profile we've been discussing.

The people who responded to Credit Karma's survey who had scores of more than 800 had some striking differences from — as well as similarities to — people lower down the credit score ladder. The average 800-plus scorer had nine open credit accounts that combined to a total of $62,481 in debt, and seven of those accounts were credit cards. They had available credit card limits of $78,377 and $5,429 in balances on those cards. When it came to payments, they made 99.99 percent of them on time, and they had zero dollars past due.

It isn't hard to sketch out what that kind of consumer looks like in real life. To have almost $80,000 in available credit, you need to have a great credit profile and a substantial income. With nine open accounts and seven credit cards, that consumer is clearly carrying a variety of high-limit cards with low balances and probably has a mortgage loan, as well as maybe a car loan. But with only $62,481 in debt, it means the person is probably mid-career and a good way toward paying off that mortgage.

You can see why a creditor would feel pretty secure doing business with that kind of customer. They have a wide variety of credit accounts, and they've performed well paying on them for a lot of years. There's very little risk there.

When you compare that composite person to the composite customer who is in the 700–799 range, you start to see where they're similar, but also very different. At this tier, the average person has seven open accounts, $125,639 in debt, six credit cards, and $7,591 in credit card debt on a credit limit of $36,199. They paid their bills on time 99.44 percent of the time and only had an average of $3 past due.

These consumers also have terrific credit, but they're carrying twice as much debt — both revolving and otherwise — on two fewer credit accounts. They're fundamentally as good at paying their bills on time and avoiding past due accounts, just like the 800-plus people are. But their utilization rate on their credit cards signals that either they're earning less money or they've historically spent more than they can afford. Don't misunderstand: they're still great risks — and profitable customers — but there's a bit more to keep an eye on.

People living in the 600s are starting to see more late payments creep into their profile, and they're carrying around a much higher percentage of debt to available credit. They have the same seven open accounts the average person in the category above them does, but they're essentially restricted from taking on more debt because of how close they are to their limits. They have an average of five credit cards and owe $7,683 on a limit of $12,194. They're late almost 5 percent of the time and have an average of $63 past due.

People in this category tend to have what I would call a "messy" credit profile. It isn't necessarily fundamentally bad, but they might have missed some payments out of carelessness, or maybe they've overlooked a medical collection over the years. A person with five credit cards is obviously still participating in the world of consumer credit, but a credit utilization of almost two-thirds available credit is a red flag to a lender that this individual is nearing their financial breaking point. Being able to just barely service the loans you have isn't a good recipe for adding more debt.

When you get to the bottom two composite borrowers, you really start to see where various factors in the credit profile work together to make somebody look like a poor financial risk. The average borrower with a score in the 500s has four open accounts, three of which are credit cards. Those credit cards are completely maxed out — $3,621 in debt, with a limit of $3,630. Lenders have basically turned off the credit spout, and the borrower is treading in water up to their nose. This borrower makes on-time payments 75 percent of the time and has an average of $283 past due.

The folks with the worst credit profiles — and scores under 500 — have gone completely upside down and owe more on their two credit cards than they have in their credit limits. In other words, they're $747 past due and have $3,520 in debt on a limit of $2,938. They're late on their payments about 40 percent of the time. With this kind of profile, people don't usually have enough income to dig themselves out of the hole and need a lifeline from a friend or relative to get out from under the penalties and high interest rates, or else they will end up declaring bankruptcy.

We obviously don't know everything just from these statistics. Income, job stability, and housing stability are important factors, but they're all highly individual and very specific. Besides, me lecturing you about making more money or doing something different with your job or housing situation isn't what this book is about.

But what we *can* talk about is how to make your financial profile look as attractive as possible today and how to make a plan to get it where you want it to be over the long haul. We talked in the last chapter about the various kinds of credit accounts that make up your score and the differences between them. Those different kinds of accounts also have different values when they're being examined by a potential creditor. The first and easiest lever for you to pull to improve your profile is to understand those differences and to engineer your mix of credit accounts in order to get as close as possible to ideal.

The Best Parking Spots at the Mall

You can think of the different kinds of credit accounts — mortgage loans, installment loans (like car and student loans), credit cards and store or merchant charge accounts, and medical debts — as parking places in the garage at the mall. True, they all serve the same purpose, but some parking spaces are better than others.

As you'll see, creditors like to see both a mix of different kinds of accounts and the right number of the "best" accounts, with the best "parking spots" being mortgages, home equity lines of credit, and so on. The entire process is very much like baking an apple pie.

Apples are an extremely important ingredient, but there are other things you need to make the crust.

① At the top of the credit account hierarchy is a mortgage account. One big reason for this is the amount of vetting that goes into getting a mortgage in the first place. All three of your credit scores are examined, along with your credit profile, and you're committing to a large loan for an extended period of time. The loan is usually collateralized more than any other loan you carry, and having a mortgage implies some stability in your location and employment. If you have a long track record of paying your mortgage on time, it's like having a highly trusted person vouch for your character.

② A home equity line of credit — a loan you take against the equity you've paid into your house — is the close relative of a mortgage and nearly counts the same when looking at a credit profile. It's obviously also tied to your most valuable asset, and demonstrating a history of taking an equity line and paying it off shows responsible behavior.

③ Installment accounts like car loans and student loans are the next most valuable pieces in the credit account hierarchy. Installment loans have a defined amount you owe and a defined amount of time in which to be repaid, so by definition, they're very stable. It's easy to analyze your performance on those loans, to see how good you've been about paying them off, and they're also a sign of income stability. As with mortgages, people are less likely to default on car loans because they represent a very important asset in getting through daily life. And most student loans carry the extra hammer of being backed by the federal government — which means you can't blow them off and have them erased in a bankruptcy. *4 (30% of Cr. Sc.)*

Credit card accounts fall in the middle for a few reasons. They're the most common accounts people have, so there's lots of data to use for comparing risk. Creditors have very sophisticated tools to measure how you use your cards — and predict how you'll use them in the future. That information is valuable to lenders when they are considering you for more credit, and it's important for lenders to be able to see that you use those kinds of revolving accounts responsibly.

But precisely because revolving accounts are open-ended and offer you the chance to spend all the way up to your credit limit, you always have the chance to defy the predictions your creditors have made for you. You can run up a huge debt almost instantly, and if you default on the loan, the lenders usually have no recourse if you choose to go through bankruptcy. Having a lot of accounts with high balances — or even a lot of them with no balances but with the potential to run up a big debt — makes you an increased risk to default in the eyes of the lender.

Medical debt is at the bottom of the credit account ladder because it's almost never discretionary and isn't tied to your income. It just isn't predictive of your financial behavior. If you have to go to the emergency room and end up with a $10,000 bill that your insurance won't pay, paying it off in installments is the only way for many people to cover that expense. Yes, there's certainly value in making timely payments — and a penalty for going into default — but those factors are taken into less consideration than other forms of debt.

This hierarchy of forms of credit is built on two foundations — risk and predictive value. Potential creditors are trying to guess how likely you are to pay them back, and they want to be able to price that risk into the loan they give you. Even a quick look at the data illustrates this point very clearly. In 2015, the foreclosure rate in the United States was at about 2 percent, while about 8 percent of all credit card balances were 90 days past due. The default rate on student loans was about 11 percent, but most of those loans were backed by the federal government, making them impossible to discharge in bankruptcy (and easier for lenders to eventually collect upon). Car loans default at about a 3 percent rate, and even subprime car loans—loans to consumers with credit scores of less than 640, which make up about a quarter of all car loans—defaulted at only about 5 percent.

Knowing the comparative value of these credit accounts, it's easy to see that a mortgage account and an installment loan in the form of a car or student loan are two important staples of the "ideal" credit profile. Beyond that, a total of five to nine loans in good standing with a mixture of mortgage loans, car loans, student loans, credit cards, and store cards comprises the profile lenders want to see. As another basis of comparison, the average American has eleven lines of credit open—which is too many. That is both saddling yourself with too much debt and hurting you in your capacity to take on a lot more of it.

Within the categories of loans themselves, individual loan accounts have more or less value depending on their characteristics. The longer you've had a loan with good payment history, the more valuable it is to your profile. This is especially important when it comes to credit cards—a subject we're going to talk more about in Chapter 7. A credit card account that adds the most value to your credit profile is one you've had for at least a year and that has a spotless payment history, so think hard before you replace a "seasoned" card with a new one.

Here's a tip: If you're trying to expand your collection of credit cards in order to come closer to the ideal profile, you're better off adding cards with great promotional rates and then moving your balances to them. But at the same time, keep your older, less competitive cards open and active so you can retain the value of the age on those accounts.

In fact, the clients in my practice with the best profiles usually follow a common credit card strategy. They have four or five cards, but two of the credit cards are the ones that do the most day-to-day duty. The other cards are stashed away and used just once or twice a month to pay a small recurring bill for something like Netflix or Spotify, and those are paid automatically. That way, all the cards show regular use and aren't closed for inactivity, but the utilization rate stays low.

Of course, if you haven't bought a home yet, you're not going to get the benefit of a mortgage loan on your profile. And when you start shopping for a home, that's the time when you're looking to improve your profile the most. Having a very clean record with your credit cards is going to be a huge help there, and you can even enhance that by going to your local bank or credit union and obtaining a small personal loan. Use the loan to pay off one of those credit cards, and make at least a year of on-time payments toward it, and you've improved your utilization rate with your credit cards *and* added an installment loan with a good record to your profile. Important: To secure a regular mortgage backed by Fannie Mae or Freddie Mac (which we'll cover in Chapter 6), you'll need two to three lines of credit open for a minimum of two years. If you don't have those, you'll be moved into a higher interest rate alternative loan no matter what your credit score is.

Be Careful with These Kinds of Loans . . .

Since we've talked about credit accounts that *do* help your profile, it's also worth noting which kinds of accounts and behaviors *don't* help. One common way people access cash is taking a loan from their 401(k) plan at work. This practice can be useful in certain circumstances, but such loans come with some big caveats.

The process is simple. Most employers have rules about if and how much employees can borrow from the vested cash in their accounts. Usually, the limits are around $20,000 and must be repaid in five years or less. (You can usually secure more flexible terms if you're using the money for a down payment on a house.) When you borrow the money, the good news is that you're paying yourself the interest over the life of the loan, and the proceeds are going back into your 401(k) account.

But there's a catch — as there is with most anything. If you change jobs, you're required to pay back the entire loan within 30 days of leaving the company, or you'll have to pay a 10 percent penalty on the remainder of the loan plus regular income tax on the total. For most people, that's a big hit.

The other caveat is that the 401(k) loan *doesn't* appear on your credit report, so paying it back — which you are required to do by way of regular automatic payments through your paycheck — doesn't give you any benefit to your credit score or your profile. This kind of loan can be a useful tool for solving short-term cash-flow problems, but it doesn't do anything for your long-term credit profile improvement strategy.

Other kinds of credit situations routinely come up for people who are struggling financially or don't have any credit score at all. Payday and title loans are designed to provide short-term cash for individuals who don't have many other options, while rent-to-own furniture stores are an option for people who wouldn't be able to finance something in the traditional way with a credit card or store card.

A payday loan is basically a cash advance on a future paycheck, and it comes with a steep price. You're usually paying $15 or $30 for every $100 borrowed, which equates to an annual interest rate of more than 700 percent on a two-week loan. You don't even get the benefit to your credit score or profile because payday lenders don't ask for credit scores to approve these loans — so they aren't reporting your performance to the credit bureaus.

Title lenders don't ask for credit scores either, which makes turning over the title to your car in order to secure a short-term loan another unprofitable way to improve your profile. Title lenders will offer you up to 50 percent of the value of your car in a short-term loan in exchange for paying a short-term interest rate of 8 to

10 percent per month. Whether or not you pay back the loan (or lose your car) also isn't reported to the bureaus.

A rent-to-own contract offers you a couch or a computer (or any other home furnishing) for a set weekly or monthly price, which also lets you own the item outright after a certain amount of time, or you can turn it back in before the term is over. Most people who do these deals can't finance a purchase in any other way. Like the payday and title loans, rent-to-own places don't do a credit check, so your good payment history isn't going to help you. And the cost to do a transaction in this way is steep. Rent-to-own companies don't charge "interest," but the weekly and monthly rates they offer for household items, when aggregated, mean you're going to end up paying three or four times the regular retail price for the item because you needed to stretch out the payment for a year or more. The truth is, scraping together some cash and buying something used off Craigslist is always going to be a better solution.

If you're in a bad financial situation and have either a low credit score or no credit score, you're not going to have a full menu of options to choose from to avoid loans like these. And if you're in a crisis and need cash this minute, you're not going to have the luxury of plotting out a multi-step strategy. But even if you do have to use one of these predatory lenders to get by for a week or a month, you need to go to Chapter 9 and follow the advice for building new credit and to get yourself back on track to rejoin the regular consumer credit marketplace, where having real choices means you can save yourself big money.

Your Credit Profile Timeline

If you start pulling these levers and moving your accounts around, how long will it take to start seeing an improvement in your profile? I tell my clients who are interested in buying a home that they need to start concentrating on their profile at least one to two years *before* they even start *shopping* for a mortgage.

Once you've started accumulating the credit accounts you need to make up the ideal profile, you'll be able to use that year to clean up the accounts you currently own so that they present in the best way possible. For credit cards, that means reducing the balances so that they're at worst no more than 20 percent of the available credit on any given card. To show off the best for creditors, you want to be even lower, at 10 percent utilization or less.

Low balances are just one part of the beauty pageant, though. You're also going to want to do what you can to reduce or eliminate what your credit report calls "derogatory items"—late payments and other delinquencies. In the next chapter, I'm going to show you exactly how to do that through negotiation and clever use of the entire consumer credit rulebook.

If your goal is to obtain the most competitive car loan or credit card introductory offer, your timeline doesn't have to advance so far out into the future. Both car lenders and credit card companies are looser with their restrictions, and they're looking for different things in your profile than what mortgage lenders are checking on.

Mortgage lenders are most concerned with your long-term ability to make a relatively large payment and whether or not the home you're buying (and the money you're contributing to the deal) will support the valuation and subsequent monthly payments. If you're trying to finance 100 percent of a deal on a house that's been appraised at 20 percent higher than any other house in the neighborhood, your mortgage lender isn't going to need to see your credit scores to decide that you won't be getting that loan. It'll be a nonstarter.

On the other hand, car lenders need to do a much higher volume of business in order to make money. And cars are significantly easier to repossess than homes. Plus, car manufacturers often contribute financing incentives that make the true cost to borrow much lower than it would otherwise be. Car lenders are looking much more at a snapshot of your credit than your overall profile and doing quick calculations to see if the income you're reporting will support the debt load you're going to be adding. Given the relatively low risk of car loan defaults, the subprime car lending business has become one of the most profitable areas for any car dealer. They're willing to take the risk on somebody with a 650 score because it means they can get a customer paying 10 or 12 percent on a loan for a car they need to get to work every day. And even if they have to take the car back, it can be resold on the used lot for an even higher margin.

One client came to me looking to qualify for a mortgage, but he had only one credit card, and his best credit score of the three was 600. He improved his score to almost 800 in less than a year by taking several of the steps you're going to read about in more detail in Chapter 6.

First, we fought with the credit bureaus to remove a handful of inaccurate items that were being reported. Then, we negotiated with several collectors that were coming after him for some medical debt and had them removed from his report. At the same time, the client broadened his credit profile by adding two authorized user accounts with the help of one of his oldest friends, and he also picked up a secured, low-limit credit card. He used it to pay his Spotify bill every month before automatically clearing it with his checking account. Lastly, he used a rent reporting website to get his great payment history on his apartment added to his credit report.

After eleven months, his credit scores had gone up almost 200 points, and his profile was looking good. He now had his choice of great loans from several banks, all at the lowest rates available on the market.

None of this work was anything heroic or tricky. True, it does take some time and willingness to use your elbows with creditors and credit bureaus that aren't particularly interested in helping you out. But with some good advice and the right plan, anybody can achieve those kinds of results. If you give yourself enough time, there's no reason why you can't have your profile polished and ready for whatever you might need.

4

....

Gaming the System

WHEN YOU SEE SOMETHING on your credit report that doesn't belong there, it should be a simple phone call to sort it out, right? You should be able to talk to a real person, and they should be able to look at your file and sort out the discrepancy in a few minutes. And everybody goes happily on their way.

Except . . . it doesn't work that way. Ever. Nothing about fighting with the credit bureaus or your creditors is easy and simple, and it's for exactly the reasons you would think. The credit bureaus are paid millions of dollars by their clients to keep track of your accounts, but *you* aren't one of those clients. The credit bureaus serve the interests of the creditors. Dealing with you and your concerns? That's just an expense.

I hear hundreds of horror stories from my clients every year, but here's just one of them. A client and friend came to me because he was in the process of moving to New York City when he got hit with a nasty surprise. A medical debt long into collections that wasn't his was showing on his credit report, so when he filled out a credit and background check application for his new place in New York, the landlord denied him.

He was sitting in the landlord's office right after getting this news when the landlord hit him with another bomb. The background check that had been run — by the same bureau — had also revealed some criminal convictions that *definitely* didn't belong to him. So in the eyes of at least one of the credit bureaus — the organizations that are responsible for telling potential creditors (and landlords) about your general responsibility level — he was a deadbeat and a criminal.

My friend came to me to try to figure out what to do. The answers are pretty simple, but unfortunately, they require a lot of legwork and a lot of persistence — which you will discover pretty quickly is the theme of this chapter.

Back in Chapter 2, where we went through what makes up the guts of your credit score, we talked about "derogatory items" — things like late payments, delinquencies, and court judgments that ding your score to different degrees. Here, we're going to talk about what to do when you discover some of those derogatory or negative items and want them to be removed.

You can certainly fight back when your credit report contains inaccuracies, but nobody is going to make that job easy. You're going to have to write and write and write, and call and call and call. Persistence and the squeaky wheel are going to be your best friends. In this chapter, I'm going to show you some of the guerilla tactics I use to help my clients get their good names (and good credit) back. Nothing we're going to talk about is illegal or even a little bit shady. But be prepared for some pushback from the companies you use these tricks on. They're not going to love you for it.

My friend with the medical collection mistake and phantom convictions? He was all fired up to call the credit bureaus and straighten them out. That's understandable, but it just doesn't work. To deal with mistakes on your credit report, you have two avenues to pursue. You can take it up with the credit bureaus — which will require you to go through a lengthy back-and-forth through the mail — or fight it through your creditors.

For starters, how the derogatory item is actually reporting on your credit report will determine a lot of how you proceed. If you have a problem with something about, say, how a credit card company has reported in the last two years, you can go directly to them. And I'm going to show you how to do that later in this chapter. But if there are items on your report that are older than two years, or they're creditors you don't recognize, or you want to preserve your right to sue if you don't get a resolution, you're going to have to deal with it through the credit bureaus. That's a big pain in the neck, and we're going to talk about that first.

Fixing a Mistake with the Bureaus

My client's mistaken-identity problem stemmed from one of the bureaus that both perform credit checks and provide criminal background information to landlords who subscribe to the service. The bureau was reporting a mystery three-year-old medical collection, as well as a long list of criminal convictions for somebody who apparently had a similar name to my client's.

After tracking down the bureau's phone number from its website, he called to dispute the information on the two reports. The representative he spoke to said there was nothing they could do over the phone and that every dispute needed to be filed either through the bureau's website or by mail — and that it would take a minimum of 30 days for the bureau to respond to any inquiry.

I can save you some time right now and tell you not to bother calling any of the bureaus with your disputes. They outsource their live customer service to India, the Philippines, and Chile, and none of those people you'll be talking to even have the ability to make any changes to your file. Their main job is to funnel you toward each bureau's dispute resolution portal on its website.

This particular bureau's online dispute form was straightforward and brief. Too brief. There was no room to fully explain what was going on and no way to attach any supporting evidence. Which is part of the plan, of course. The bureaus want to make it as easy as possible to deny a dispute by saying you didn't provide enough information for your claim.

That left using the mail. And if you're going to dispute something with the bureaus, the mail is the only way of moving forward. But even that process isn't as straightforward as you might think.

All the bureaus use an automated dispute resolution process called e-OSCAR to respond to disputes mailed in by consumers. When you type up your letter and mail it, it gets opened, scanned, and categorized by machines. The software spits out a two- or three-character code that represents the category of your dispute and sends it (along with a brief summary of your dispute language) to the creditor to verify the information. The creditor then replies to the bureau, confirming the information or stating that there's been some kind of mistake.

It won't be surprising to learn that you don't have much of a chance with the machine. Your overall goal, of course, is to get your dispute kicked out of the automated character reading machine and processed by a real person. The easiest way to do it — and I'm not making this up — is to handwrite your dispute letter on paper that is some other color than white. A nice, legible cursive is great for the job. You want the bureau employee to be able to understand what you're saying — just not the computer.

My friend got his credit report from the bureau that was claiming he had the medical collection debt, and he mailed in his dispute as I suggested. He requested that the bureau verify his debt — meaning the creditor had to respond with identifying information that proves my friend was the one who signed up for the debt.

In about five weeks, he received a letter back saying that his dispute was rejected, but he didn't get any reason for it. Again, that's not surprising. When a creditor gets your dispute from the credit bureau, it uses its own automated system to check on it, and it almost always only uses the information it already has in its computers — you know, the information that was wrong in the first place — to verify. The supporting evidence you sent in? It may or may not get considered. It's impossible to know, because when you get your response, you don't get any context for the decision.

So my client had to write another dispute letter with more backing evidence and threatened to sue the credit bureau if it didn't remove the false item from his report. Not only was the medical collection attributed to somebody with a different middle initial, but it was from a time when he could verify through his medical insurance records that he hadn't even set foot in a hospital.

Another five weeks later, he finally received the letter he was looking for — one that said the collection was being removed from his account. By now, three months had passed, and he was living in a month-to-month sublet while he tried to get it sorted out. The truth is, he was actually lucky. The back-and-forth with the letter writing can go on for months, with weeks and weeks in between communication. It often lasts so long that, in our office, we refer to the letter exchanges as "rounds" — as in, we're in Round 3 with Experian or TransUnion.

Winning the battle over the erroneous medical collection debt was only part of the war, too. He had to do an entirely separate and parallel dispute process with the same bureau about the mismerged court records. For those records, he started by calling the court that was listed on the records to see if it could give him more information. It was a court in a city he'd never been to, in a state he'd never visited. The response he got from the court was, unfortunately, typical. The vast majority of courts in the United States don't forward information to the credit bureaus. It just isn't one of their priorities. But data aggregators like LexisNexis *do* scrape that information from court records and sell it on to the bureaus, which then market it to landlords and employers for background checks.

It doesn't take too much imagination to see what happens. During the process of scraping the records, transferring them to the bureaus, and assigning them to different credit reports, mistakes occasionally get made. The papers can be scanned wrong. It could be a keystroke error from the courthouse, the aggregator, or the credit bureau. But millions of people are walking around with bad information tagged to their credit report, and the only party with the incentive to pay attention and do something about it is you.

If you think it's problematic that the credit bureaus were accepting information on liens and civil judgments for use in calculating your credit scores without cross-checking the information, you're not alone. In July 2017, the bureaus finally agreed to vet the information more closely — and if liens or judgments do not include name and address and either a Social Security number or date of birth, they will be excluded from credit reports provided by Equifax, Experian, and TransUnion. This isn't a small adjustment: virtually all civil judgments and about half of tax liens do not meet this criteria, and more than ten million consumers probably saw some kind of score improvement in the months immediately after the change.

By the way, once you do get that letter that says a mistake has been corrected, you might be tempted to count on the rules — which say that the bureau fixing the mistake has to notify all the other bureaus to make sure the mistake doesn't appear elsewhere. Don't rely upon that. Send a copy of the letter, along with your own letter (by mail, not email), to the other two bureaus, letting them know you've resolved this dispute and that it should not appear on their versions of your report.

In a day and age when most communication happens through email, you're probably going to get pretty tired of stamping and mailing stuff, but every time you close an envelope, feel good about the fact that you're not getting pushed off your goal just because the bureaus want to put some steep obstacles in your way.

Fixing a Mistake with a Creditor

When you're dealing with smaller dollar figures and more recent blemishes, it can make sense to go to the actual creditor instead of the credit bureau — especially if your account is still active and hasn't been passed on to a collection agency. The tactics we're going to talk about here are useful when you have the chance to deal with real people over the phone and when there are sensitive matters like medical collection debts that deal with what can be confidential information.

For the same reasons credit card companies are constantly trying to poach clients from their competitors, the company you bank with will (within reason) try to make you happy so that you'll stay, especially if it's something easy to do. When I'm working with clients who are trying to fix their credit issues, some of the first "low-hanging fruit" we go after are single instances of a late payment on a credit card that is otherwise in good standing.

I'll give you an example. Say you've been with Citibank for ten years, and the only late payment you have is from a year ago. That blemish, by itself, isn't going to do much damage to your score. But if you have other collection issues you're trying to deal with, any little bit you can fix helps.

Because of your long-term, productive relationship with Citi, you can call them up and simply ask them to remove the derogatory item. You don't have to admit guilt over the phone. In effect, you're basically trying to trade on the goodwill of the company to do you a favor.

The first response you get (and keep in mind that credit card companies log all of your calls with them, so they know the last time you checked in) will probably be some form of "We can't do that" or "It's illegal for us to go back and change that."

Nonsense. They *can* change those things, and they do. You just need to be politely persistent. If you don't get satisfaction, call again and ask to speak to a supervisor. If you're persistent enough, you'll usually get the blemish removed — mostly because doing so will make you go away. Again, I'm not talking about doing this when you have a terrible payment record. This is for a situation where you have an isolated problem with a company with which you've had a long, positive relationship.

What happens when things aren't so good? There are some other strategies you can try, but you obviously don't have as much leverage. As we've been discussing, the credit card companies want to lend you as much money as possible at the highest interest rate while still leaving you able to pay it back. They know that if they have to go to collections with you, they'll probably only collect pennies on the dollar. So if you run into a problem — say, you've lost your job or you took a new job that pays much less — you can often negotiate to get some short-term relief.

For example, let's say you have $15,000 in debt on a credit card, and you don't see being able to make that minimum payment for a few months. You can write your creditor a letter asking for what is called a "forbearance" — a temporary suspension of the minimum payment requirements. Now, this doesn't remove any of your debt. It just stops the clock for a predetermined period of time to let you get back on your feet. What you say in your forbearance letter matters. Telling a creditor you had to take six weeks of unpaid leave from work but will be back soon on full status, or that you're having a temporary financial setback because of a divorce, is encouraging. Saying you've lost your job and have no prospects for a new one, or that you just got hit with a $50,000 medical bill, isn't. The creditor can decide whether to grant the forbearance or not, and if it does, it will usually be for a period of two to four months. Your access to credit on that account will usually be suspended while you are in forbearance, and when the term ends, your minimums will pick up where they left off — plus the accrued interest.

If you've reached the point where you just won't be able to pay, you have some other avenues to try before you let the account go into collections. Again, the creditor isn't thrilled to have to charge off your debt after 120 days and get only pennies for it, so there's a sweet spot between the amount you owe, the amount you could offer to settle the debt, and the time that has passed since you were current. If you're only 45 days late, your creditor is going to continue to try and motivate you with the punishment of black marks on your credit in order to make you current. But if it's been 90 or 120 days and you still haven't paid, those black marks are already there, and the creditor will probably be willing to negotiate.

In that negotiation, your strongest position is to offer a lump sum settlement for the debt. Say you owe that $15,000. You can offer to pay the creditor $7,500 in exchange for the entire debt being settled. If the creditor perceives that it isn't likely to get much more than that, it will often take the offer. There's no real rule of thumb about how much to offer to make a creditor accept. It's a negotiation, and the surrounding factors are going to play a big part. If your creditor takes a look at your credit report and sees all kinds of problems with other creditors, it will probably be more willing to work with you because you could well end up declaring bankruptcy and leave the creditor with nothing. But if you have otherwise decent credit and ask your creditor to take a $5,000 or $10,000 haircut, you probably aren't going to get the answer you want.

If you do come to a settlement agreement, it's important to know the consequences of it. Your account will be closed, and the creditor will report to the bureaus that you settled for less than was owed. That will punish your score, but not as severely as a bankruptcy. It will hurt more in the short term than a collection, but it means the issue has now been resolved and recedes. A collection you don't deal with can stay in your report for years, hurting your score. You'll also have to check with your tax person to find out what your liability is to the IRS. Forgiven debt is considered income, and you'll usually have to pay the applicable tax.

All the strategies I've been discussing will work with any creditor — not just a credit card company. There might be some differences in the mechanism you use, but the overall approach is similar. You can use the information on the next few pages to find the specific plan you need for other kinds of creditors, such as mortgage originators and car lenders. (For more information on how to deal with student loan issues, go to Chapter 10.)

Dealing with Debt Collectors

Once an account has gone delinquent, it's only a matter of time before the creditor to which you owe the money sells off the debt to a collection agency. That collection agency buys the debt for a fraction of what you owe, but it then keeps anything it collects from you.

Having a collection isn't anything to be ashamed about. It happens sometimes when you can't pay a bill because of unforeseen life events, but it can also happen without you even knowing it. One of the favorite strategies of debt-collecting companies is to purchase a large portfolio of debt and simply go through and quietly add each individual debt to the credit reports of the people in that database they just bought. They won't bother to send you any letters or try to collect from you. They're just waiting for you to notice problems with your credit scores and discover where those issues are arising. Then, most people will come running to try to settle the debt — especially if it isn't for a lot of money. It's shady, but perfectly legal for them to do it, as long as the debt is legitimately yours.

Of course, other collection efforts are a lot more aggressive. You can get stern letters demanding repayment and barrages of phone calls from collectors who will literally say anything to try to get you to pay them something. But before you become intimidated into forking over your debit card number so they can clean you out, you

60

need to take some precautions to make sure you're settling these financial problems, once and for all.

First, you have the right to tell any collector who calls you on the phone that the only way you will respond is via a written letter. Ask for their address and send them a letter stating that you will not respond to any telephone calls. If they try to call again after your warning, just remind them that they're in violation of the Fair Debt Collection Practices Act and that you can sue them.

Your next step is to make sure that the debt these collectors are chasing is both yours and still valid. By checking your credit report, you can confirm that the claims from the collector truly match up to what you're seeing on your report. If a collector demands cash settlement for some credit card bill you had ten years ago, the clock has already run out on that debt, and you are not obligated to pay it. (Be sure to check the laws in your state to see what the statute of limitations is on a creditor's ability to sue you for an unpaid debt. It ranges from three to ten years, depending on the state.)

Of course, not all debt collectors are going to look at the debt they've purchased in bulk and say, "Gee, this person's debt is a month past expiration. We'd better strike it from our books." What really happens is that collectors simply try to collect on *all* the debt they've purchased, and if you're foolish enough (or pressured enough) to pay up on an eleven-year-old debt, well, that's on you. In basic terms, the seven-year window is the timeframe that items have to show up in your credit report, and it's also the same timeframe you're looking at for creditors to be able to pressure you for a certain debt, at least when it comes to being able to hurt your score. In other words, if somebody is coming after you for a run-of-the-mill credit card debt outside that seven-year window, whether or not you settle it is not going to affect your credit score, and in many cases, you're not legally obligated to pay. However, specific kinds of debt, like federally backed student loans and court judgments, never expire.

If you look on your credit report and don't see the debt that's being referenced by the collection agency, you can send a letter demanding that it "verifies" the debt before you pay anything. The agency needs to prove that it acquired the debt from somebody with proof that you were the one who took out that loan or signed for the credit card. That verification comes in the form of a name, Social Security number, address, account number, last payment date, and full name of the original creditor on the amount you owe.

According to a Federal Trade Commission study published in 2013, only about 50 percent of the debt that consumers ask to be verified actually is verified by the collection agencies that own it. This happens for a number of reasons. The older the debt becomes, the more often it has been transferred from collection agency to collection agency — for an average transaction price of about four cents per dollar of debt being purchased.

If you defaulted on your American Express account three months ago, the first collection agency to buy that debt paid the highest premium for it because the information is fresh. It knows right where to find you, and it has the leverage of being fresh in your mind. Plus, you know you owe the money (assuming it wasn't a mistake on your report!), and you're vulnerable to being pushed into settling it.

But, after a certain amount of time has passed, a collector that isn't able to collect from you will sell your debt on to another collector that specializes in "long shots." It buys collections accounts by the tens of thousands for pennies on the dollar and only needs to convert a few of them in order to make a healthy return on its investment.

As your debt gets older and gets sold further down the line, the companies who have purchased the debt don't have much invested in it. They aren't usually going to want to go through the expense of verifying it if you request that, and, as a result, they're likely to just write it off.

62

Because each collector has less and less invested, they're also increasingly more likely to be willing to make a deal. For example, if you have an old department store account that went into collections five years ago for a $500 debt, the third or fourth collection company that bought your debt might only have a couple of bucks into it. If you offer to settle the debt for a fraction of the original dollar figure, it could still well be a big profit for the collector.

However you decide to negotiate, you have to start from the position that you will not settle unless you get a letter stipulating that the debt will be *removed* from your credit report when you pay the agreed-upon settlement. Don't be fooled if the collector says it will put a note on your account saying that you paid. A note doesn't do anything to affect the underlying score or the impact that late payment has on your score. *You want nothing less than a removal of the collection.*

What are the stakes if you don't pay or settle? Well, every month that collection reports on your credit, you will get hit with another penalty. Your score will continue to drop until you do something about it. At worst, you want to pay something to get it settled, even if the agency won't remove the derogatory hit.

Medical debt requires a different kind of strategy. It's different than any other debt on your record in that the information contained in your file can be highly sensitive. It can contain information about who your doctors are, what you've been treated for, and the record of your care. Those pieces of information are strongly protected by the Health Insurance Portability and Accountability Act. One of the foundations of HIPAA is that nobody can talk about your health information unless you give them written authorization.

A 2016 study done by the *New York Times* and the Kaiser Family Foundation found that in the last year, 20 percent of Americans had medical bills they struggled to pay. That's a lot of people sweating over some big numbers and a lot of creditors and collection agencies coming after delinquent payments.

If you're behind on your payments to your original medical creditor — say, the hospital where you got your broken leg fixed in the emergency room — it has all the paperwork you signed when you checked in, allowing access to your medical records.

But if you don't pay your bill with that creditor and it sells that debt on to a collection agency, the collection agency doesn't have the same rights to your private medical information. Unless you sign a different form for the collector, the only thing it can talk to you about is the dollar figure you owe.

This can put a poorly trained debt collection cold caller in a bad position. If you get one of those calls for collection, you're perfectly within your rights to ask the caller what the nature of the debt was and whether they can give you more information about it so you can figure out what you're supposed to pay.

If the collector is dense enough to start rattling off identifying information (and you're recording it on your phone in a state where one-party phone recording is OK), that collection agency has just violated HIPAA in a bad way.

Your next move is to write a letter to the collection agency stating what happened and that you have recorded proof. You can then offer to forget about the HIPAA violation in exchange for debt forgiveness — and for the collection agency scratching your debt from the record.

When you check your credit report, you need to be extremely diligent about examining any medical debt or collections you may have. Many, many people have medical bills they never even knew had accumulated. Curiously, this happens most frequently to people with medical insurance. They go to the hospital and get something taken care of, and later down the line, the insurance company decides not to pay for all of it. The hospital then sends out a bill for the remainder. Because of the blizzard of paperwork that comes out of being in the hospital, those bills — which are often for very small amounts of money, like $100 or $150 — can get lost. But when they show up later as a collection, that $100 unpaid bill hits your credit scores hard.

Your Action Plan

Whether or not you are currently in a bad situation with one of the credit bureaus, a creditor, or a collector, you can take some proactive steps to protect yourself.

1. Request a credit report from one bureau every four months. By rotating the bureaus, over the course of a year, you will see everything going on with your credit as far as the three bureaus are concerned. Some creditors space out their reporting, or they don't report to all three bureaus. If you don't create some space between the requests and monitor all three on a pattern, you could well miss some activity.

2. Once you have your reports, write to each of the three bureaus and request that old, outdated addresses, phone numbers, and employers be removed from your report. The only pieces of information *required* on your report are your name, Social Security number, and current address. By removing old addresses, you're actually taking away a valuable tool for collectors with old debt to track you down. Creditors and collectors will often only be able to associate data tied to your address. If you remove the old ones, they won't be able to tie some of those debts to you. If it's a collector down the stream who bought your account as one of thousands on a basic spreadsheet, they will just move onto the next one.

3. Send a letter to each of the hospitals and medical offices you deal with, stating specifically that you're opting out of any

HIPAA-authorized disclosure of your protected medical information — which includes name, address, Social Security number, payment information, and treatment procedures — to anybody besides yourself and your attorney. Also specify that you do not authorize the disclosure of any protected information to any family members or for notification. You're establishing that you will be the only conduit of your medical information and the financial information tied to it.

4. Identify those key items in your reports that are causing the most negative impact and try to resolve them first. Generally speaking, late payments and delinquencies in the last two years are going to hurt your scores more than anything else. If you can take care of some of those blemishes, you're going to get the most bang for your buck.

5. Clip the low-hanging fruit. You can improve your scores just by doing some of the basic cleanup we've been talking about — like reducing your credit card balances. If you have collections for small amounts and the creditors won't settle for less than you owe, bite the bullet and send the check to get them removed from your report.

6. Add positives when you can. Becoming an authorized user on an account is a nice positive, as is adding in other data that isn't always considered on a report. I've had clients use RentReporters.com very successfully to get their positive rental payment history included on their credit report. If you can show you've been paying rent on time for seven years, that's a positive for you.

Given what I do for a living, one of the first questions I get when I'm giving a presentation or a seminar is "When is it time to bring in a professional?" With the tools in this book, you're going to be able to handle many situations on your own. But if you're uncomfortable negotiating on the phone and dealing with some pushback from creditors, you should consider letting a professional help. That's especially true when you're dealing with complex issues with serious legal ramifications, like potential bankruptcies and foreclosures, tax liens, and court judgments. Fumbling a negotiation for a few hundred dollars isn't the end of the world, but getting yourself in deeper with the court system can have real consequences.

5

....

The Five Biggest Credit Mistakes and How to Avoid Them

I'VE HEARD EVERY STORY.

Some of them are big, complicated ones from famous people with a lot of moving parts to their personal finances. And a lot of them are regular, everyday problems that pretty much everybody has along the way.

Like the multimillionaire owner of a minority share of one of the most famous sports teams in the world. He became a client because he was trying to figure out why he was having so much trouble qualifying for a reasonable rate on a large mortgage he was trying to take on an apartment he was buying — an apartment he could have paid for in cash, easily.

It turned out that he was being derailed because he was very close to the $500 limit on a gas card he had given to one of his drivers. Just like that, an accounting oversight on a $500 line of credit dinged his score to the point where he looked like a questionable credit risk — and set him up to pay tens of thousands of dollars more in interest on a potential loan.

In the same transaction, he made two of the most common mistakes anybody can make. He applied for a new loan without knowing the full picture of his credit report, and he underestimated how various issues could affect his scores.

Another client came in trying to put the pieces back together after getting all the way to the closing table and then having a bank pull out of a conditional mortgage agreement.

What happened?

Before the closing, the client went out and picked up one of those no-interest, pay-it-off-in-six-months company credit cards from Home Depot to stock her new house with appliances. But that new credit line threw the client's debt ratios out of whack, and she no longer qualified for the loan for which she had been conditionally approved.

These two real-world examples had big, messy consequences, but I chose them to illustrate an important point.

My job here isn't to make you feel good about your personal credit situation. It's to show you how to *fix* your problems — and *avoid* those problems in the first place.

I'm going to run down the list of the five biggest credit potholes *every* consumer faces. It doesn't matter if you have seven figures of net worth in your various accounts or if you're somebody just starting out in the work world and are looking for a cheap lease on a small car.

*

Here's the bottom line: if you avoid these five mistakes — or use the information in this chapter to dig yourself out of trouble more quickly — your credit scores will be substantially better because of it.

Mistake No. 1

Walking into a negotiation for a mortgage, car loan, or other big-ticket line of credit without knowing exactly where your credit score stands.

*

Let me ask you a personal question.

Think about the last time you bought something decently expensive online. Let's say, something more than $200. How much time did you spend comparing prices at different websites, checking shipping costs, and generally doing your research before you bought?

I bet it was more than thirty minutes' worth of surfing and comparing. That isn't much time, but it's still more time than most people spend getting ready to spend the most money they're ever going to spend on a single big item in their lives — either a home or a car.

During the home-buying or car-buying process, people usually shop around for what they want, and when they find it, they then enter the domain of the "finance person" — either a mortgage broker or a finance manager at a car dealership.

But they go in there with next to no information about their credit situation and no way of evaluating whether the terms of the loan they're being offered are bad, mediocre, or good. I know this because I saw it firsthand in my ten years as a mortgage originator — and see it today in the hundreds of conversations I have with clients every month.

The result?

People then find themselves being pressed into making a decision about a huge amount of money in a short period of time, and they do it with the least amount of research and preparation compared to almost *anything* they buy.

It makes no sense.

Before we even get to how to improve your score in preparation for applying for a mortgage (which is covered in full in the next chapter), just knowing where you stand *before* you shop is a good place to start.

After all, how do you know if the rate you're being offered matches your credit score tier? If the mortgage broker tells you

you're in the middle tier and you don't know where you stand, you're just taking his or her word for it.

Bear in mind that a difference of just 10 or 20 points in your score can add up to hundreds of dollars in additional interest payments in just one month on a home or car loan. That's a penalty of *tens of thousands of dollars* over the life of a thirty-year mortgage on a $250,000 home. On a car, it can easily be a $150 monthly difference in payment — enough to put gas in the tank for the entire year.

You wouldn't be that careless if you were going online to buy a $600 television. Don't do it when you're making the biggest of big-ticket purchases.

At the minimum, get your real credit report and a full understanding of your credit scores from all three bureaus six months before you intend to make one of those big purchases. Then, make an honest assessment of your assets, and figure out exactly how much cash you're going to contribute to the deal in the form of a down payment. Once you do that, you can use one of the popular online mortgage or car loan calculators to get a ballpark estimate of what your interest rates, monthly payments, and taxes will be. That will give you some parameters to shop with when you sit down with the broker or loan specialist.

Trust me. It's far better than walking in from the cold and just hoping for the best.

Mistake No. 2

Putting off understanding or dealing with your credit situation.

*

Nobody likes bad news. But your financial life works a lot like your car's condition. Serious issues don't usually go away if you just ignore them.

And when it comes to credit, many people don't want to look under the hood, so to speak, because they're afraid of what they'll see. They'll be confronted with credit card debt they don't want to think about, or they'll see a record of some of the bad financial decisions they've made over the years.

In the case of something really damaging, like a bankruptcy, it's easy to lapse into feeling like there's nothing you can do anyway, so why even bother?

This is totally understandable, but it's also keeping you from actually solving your problems.

And there are solutions for *anything*. I see examples in my practice every day. Clients who have gone through bankruptcy have successfully gotten back into the credit card market six months after and, a few months after that, were able to get a car loan. Seven years later, their credit score can look like it never took a hit.

Of course, if you're like most people, you're not in a credit crisis, but you have things that need regular attention. And the more quickly you give them your attention, the easier (and less painful) the remedies are.

For example, even after a bankruptcy, you can dip your toe in the credit waters by getting a secured card (which we'll talk more about in Chapter 11). That secured card, with some good behavior, can turn into a conventional card, which can then be the ladder you use to pull yourself out of your scoring hole.

With identity theft at an all-time high (and getting worse by the day), remaining ignorant of your credit situation also exposes you to greater risk of getting compromised by a hacker or thief. If you aren't aware on at least a week-to-week basis where you stand with different accounts, you could be getting ripped off for weeks and months before you even discover the violation. The phony transactions can usually be reversed if found within the first few months, but not without a lot of headaches and time.

It's almost impossible to make your personal data totally safe, but with some attention, you can make it way harder for the thieves to steal your stuff.

One cold, hard fact should make all of this more real to you.

Whether you like it or not, you're always going to need to be part of the credit universe. You need a credit score to buy life insurance, and your credit is often used to screen you for a job or a rental apartment. And it's extremely difficult to navigate the modern world without a credit card. Just try buying a plane ticket or renting a hotel room or car without one.

Whatever your score is, you're going to have to deal with the consequences of it almost every day. If you're having trouble, you might as well take the steps to fix it. You need to get back on that horse. If you don't and just stay in denial, you'll wake up five years later and *still* be in the hole.

And even worse, you'll still have to do the same work to get out.

Mistake No. 3

Underestimating the ways various negatives hurt your credit score — and how seemingly unimportant factors can help it.

*

By now, you shouldn't be surprised that a lot of things about the way credit bureaus determine your score aren't totally logical.

One especially big one? The way in which delinquencies are accounted for on your record.

Believe it or not, if you're delinquent on a credit card on which you owe $100, the black mark is the same as if you're delinquent on one on which you owe $10,000. Your score might be affected in other ways by the balances you carry, but your delinquencies all count the same, no matter how much money is at stake.

This is an extremely important factor to remember because there's no such thing as a "minor" delinquency. If you forget to make even a small payment and it's to a creditor that reports to the bureau, it counts the same as skipping a car payment.

Worse yet, the punishment you receive for those delinquencies is much more painful if you have a high score when it happens.

In other words, if you have a pristine 780 credit rating, a delinquency on even the smallest thing — say, a $45 medical collection you didn't know anything about — can crush you by up to 50 or 75 points immediately. In contrast, if your credit score is mediocre to begin with, say 680, the same hit might only cost you 20 points.

Why?

Because a credit rating is designed to calculate risk and predict what that risk might be over the next two years. So if you're a person with a 680 score, a lot of that risk is already priced in. If you're a 780 who is all of a sudden missing a bunch of payments (even if they're small ones), your situation has suddenly changed.

This is why you need to be extremely thorough when you review your credit report, and you need to be vigilant about checking it at least annually. It isn't enough just to keep track of your big payments — the mortgage, car, and school loans — and feel like you're insulated from any damage to your score.

On the flip side, you're probably doing some seemingly mundane "housekeeping" things that are costing you chances at a higher score. It's always good to keep track of the interest rates on your credit cards and shop around for better deals. But flipping cards does have one serious downside.

The length of your credit history counts for 15 percent of your credit score, and that length is computed by examining your accounts for age. It's great that you've paid that school loan on time for two years, but a credit card that has been in good standing with no late payments for ten years (or longer) is pure gold.

Many people will go through their accounts and see a low-limit card they don't use any more and abruptly cancel it. But the truth is, those long-term accounts are like old friends who can vouch for you. They tell the bureaus that you have been responsible for a long time.

It doesn't sound like much, but the simple act of cancelling that card can penalize you to the point where you don't qualify for the highest tier of credit — and you haven't done anything "bad" to change your profile except show an assemblage of accounts that are newer. In fact, the damage can be just as bad as if you had a 60-day delinquency.

The "age" factor is why mortgage accounts are so powerful on your credit report. They're the loans that people tend to take out for a considerable amount of time, and they're also usually one of the first bills that gets paid every month. I'm not suggesting that you pass up a chance to refinance your home loan if you can get a historically low rate — but you definitely want to keep in mind the overall impact on your credit score if you're giving up a loan account that you've had established for a long time.

Mistake No. 4

Not paying attention to the mix and timing of your new credit applications.

*

It's a cliché, but timing really is everything. Especially with credit scores.

You probably want to wait until you start that hot new job with the big salary before you commit to the higher rent or mortgage payment. And waiting until you pay off that school loan is probably a good strategy before signing up for a big car lease payment.

But even though many people intuitively understand the concept of timing, they don't have a good handle on how adding and subtracting lines of credit affects their scores. And that leaves them open for receiving a nasty surprise.

The example I discussed at the beginning of the chapter is only one of the most obvious ones. If you think of your credit score as a wheelbarrow, your score indicates the total weight of the rocks you could fit in the cart. By going out and adding a line of credit from a home store, my client was actually adding small rocks to the cart *before* she made sure the biggest and most important rock (e.g., the mortgage) fit.

That's why it's so important to follow the ideal mix of credit lines we talked about in Chapter 2. Adding new credit lines that don't help your score — and that you don't really need — is just hurting how you're going to be judged on the lines that *do* matter.

In the example at the beginning of this chapter, my client didn't get her mortgage because of the new debt she added. But damage that isn't fatal can still be extremely painful. You can easily hurt your credit score by 10 points by adding another credit line. Fall from the top tier, above 740 or 760 (depending on the lender), to the middle tier and you'll end up paying 2 percentage points more on a loan. That translates into $300 more on a mortgage payment *per month* and $100,000 more interest paid over the life of the loan.

*

Even people who do have some awareness of this issue still get snagged when they rely on a "pretend" credit score like the ones you get from Credit Karma or some other unofficial source.

Let me explain. Let's say you get a promotion from your credit card company and it offers you a free look at your "credit score." What you're getting isn't the real thing, but a "consumer education report." In my experience, what those "pretend" reports are really designed to do is educate you right out of your money — by influencing you to apply for more lines of credit by suggesting your situation in rosier terms than is real.

Why does this matter?

Because the bureaus and credit card companies are obviously interested in hitting you for the highest rates possible *while still approving you to get a line of credit*. They *want* you to have the card, the car, and the mortgage, but they also want you to pay as much as possible for the money.

One thing Credit Karma in particular *is* good for is the credit estimator tool it has on its website. You obviously want to take the score it gives you with a grain of salt, but the estimator tool lets you plug in certain scenarios — like cancelling or adding a line of credit — and see how that would affect your score. It isn't official, but it will give you a rough estimate of what will happen.

Mistake No. 5

Failing to deal with your credit issues using a coherent strategy and approach.

*

You're a reasonable, honest person, right?

If you're standing in line at the grocery store and you see the woman in front of you drop a $20 bill from her wallet, you probably pick it up and give it back to her, right?

That's the reflex response of most people — and it's also the one that gets most of us in much deeper trouble with the credit bureaus than is necessary.

How so?

When most people get a letter from a collection agency about a legitimate bill they didn't realize they owed — say, a medical expense from a hospital stay a few years ago that didn't end up getting covered by insurance — the natural response is to reach for the checkbook and pay it.

But paying that bill before taking very specific steps is like dropping another bomb on your credit.

Remember, the damage to your credit score is already there from the missed payments and collection action. Paying the bill without a coherent strategy just makes the damage larger and more recent.

As discussed in Chapter 2, the bureaus use a combination of your payment history and credit card usage to determine your score. The more recent the activity on your account, the more it factors into your score. If you've made the last three years of payments on your car loan on time, that is going to show up even more powerfully in your score than the late payment you had four years ago.

In most cases, credit reports compile the last seven years of information on you. If that letter you got from the creditor is about an incident from four or five years ago, those missed payments have been hurting you all along — but ironically, have been hurting you *less* as more time has passed.

Paying that bill now rips the scab off the wound, so to speak. Settling the debt will suddenly put a big new mark on your score.

I'm not suggesting you ditch your obligations and ignore the bill if it's a legitimate one. You can and should resolve it, but take care to do it following these specific steps.

First, make sure the bill *is* a legitimate one. Plenty of people have the same name, similar addresses, and other comparable identifying information. Now is the time to make sure the Joe A. Smith the creditor is trying to track down is really you and not another one who lives in your town. Or, the bill could represent a legitimate debt, but it's one you've paid — and you have proof you paid.

If the creditor is calling you about the debt, tell them you aren't responding to anything until you see it in writing and make them send you a letter summarizing the debt. You can then compare it to your records and go to your credit report to see if the information (and the delinquency) matches.

If the debt isn't yours, or it's one you've already paid, you can dispute it with both the creditor and the credit bureaus themselves.

But OK, let's say the debt is legitimate, and it's time to deal with it.

Just keep one important item in mind. Collection agencies aren't exactly known for their ethics. They're not interested in your sad stories, and they aren't going to help you sort out a "misunderstanding." The way their business works is they buy up millions of dollars of uncollected debts for pennies on the dollar from hospitals, department stores, and other organizations and then hire a bunch of mostly untrained workers to try to bully and shame as many people as possible into paying up.

Or, an agency will take a sneakier route. It buys up the old debt and then hits your credit report with a delinquency. Then, it waits. It knows that once you see it on your report — most likely when you're getting ready to go borrow money for something important — you're going to come to it first to try to resolve the debt.

You want to tell the collection agency right away that you'll work with them to settle the debt, but you're going to do it on your terms.

The most important rule? Don't count on anything you hear over the phone with a worker at a collection agency. Their job is to shake money from you, and they'll do it any way they can. They'll use guilt, threats, persistence — you name it. They can promise to do all sorts of things, but none of it matters unless it's in *writing*.

Your goal is to discuss establishing a plan to pay off the debt in exchange for written confirmation that the delinquency will definitely be *deleted* from your credit report. You'll probably get pushback from the creditor — it will say it isn't allowed to delete it, or it will send you a letter that says you paid in full but not that the delinquencies will be removed — but in the end, it's getting paid, so it'll play ball.

Here is an example of a letter that has worked for my clients:

Nov. 20, 2016

To Whom It May Concern:

This letter serves as confirmation that, upon receipt of $356.20, account 12345678 will be marked as paid in full and deleted from the three major credit bureaus, Experian, Equifax, and TransUnion.

Please be aware that this is not an acknowledgment or acceptance of the debt, as I have not received any verification of the debt. Neither is this a promise to pay, nor is this a payment agreement unless you provide a response as detailed below.

I am aware that your company has the ability to report this debt to the credit bureaus as you deem necessary. Furthermore, you have the ability to change the listing since you are the information furnisher. As granted by the Fair Debt Collection Practices Act, I have the right to dispute this alleged debt. If I do not receive your postmarked response within 15 days, I will withdraw the offer and request full verification of this debt.

Once you have your letter in response from the creditor — have it emailed to you as a PDF — you can pay the debt, but be sure to go in 30 days after and verify on your credit report that the delinquency has been removed. If it hasn't, you can use the letter from the creditor along with proof of payment and dispute the delinquency with the credit bureaus.

And if the creditor still won't play ball?

If it won't deal with you, wait a few months. Your debt will probably be moved to a different company — which bought it at even more of a discount — and you can try the process again. The next company will probably be more in the mood to settle with you because it has less invested in it.

Again, it's important to keep in mind where on that seven-year debt clock your debt collection sits. Be cautious with debts that are four years and older, because paying them without making arrangements for deletion will hurt your credit score. How much? A fresh notification on a five-year-old debt creates the same pain as a brand new delinquency — a 50-point whack to your credit score in some cases.

6

....

Preparing Your Credit Score for a New Home Purchase

IT'S 1970.

You decide it's time to become a homeowner for the first time.

For the purpose of this conversation, you're perfectly average in every way. You make the average income, $3,900, you're buying the average $23,000 house, and you have the average 25 percent to use as a down payment — $5,750 — which you probably got from a relative.

To get a mortgage for the rest, you go down to your local bank and meet in person with a loan officer, who goes over your complete financials — job history and income, savings and checking accounts, and credit cards (although, in 1970, most people had only one or two department store or gas cards).

After that relatively simple process, you signed up for a thirty-year adjustable-rate mortgage that ended up being about a 3-point spread from the prime rate, which in 1970 was 7 percent. That 10 percent mortgage had an initial payment of $150 a month.

Fast-forward to the present.

It won't surprise you to learn that things are not just more expensive these days, but also a lot more complicated.

If you're average today, you make $56,000, and your home costs

$350,000. The average down payment on a home is now around 14 percent — or $49,000 — and the process to get a mortgage involves a much more invasive procedure with people you may not ever meet in person. You'll get to argue and plead with your Realtor, a mortgage broker, and a multinational bank's India-based customer service representative.

And, after all that, you might not even get the loan. Since the great financial recession of 2008–09, more than 70 percent of all mortgage applications are rejected — up from about 25 percent a decade ago.

But wait — maybe you're not average.

Let's say you own your own business, and you're making $175,000. You use credit cards to pay for your business expenses, and you pay them off them at least quarterly. Or maybe you're making $600,000, and you have the extravagant lifestyle to prove it. You have a $1,000 car payment, $5,000 rent on a condo, and pretty substantial credit card debt, but you get a big bonus every January, and you get along just fine.

A mortgage should be no problem, right? At least on paper, this should be a no-brainer.

Actually, my office is filled with high-net-worth clients every week who get a rude awakening in the form of a mortgage application rejection. Most of them say the same thing: "I have a million in cash sitting in the bank. Why am I getting turned down for a mortgage?" The answer is the same for an NBA player or a platinum-selling recording artist as it is for the average person.

When a lender is considering your loan application, the most important thing is your *credit score.* Not income. Bonuses. Popularity. Twitter followers. Hit records. Points per game. None of that stuff matters. ✦✦✦✦✦✦

Loan standards these days are higher than ever, fewer loans are being written, and there are 75 percent fewer companies in the business of providing mortgages than even five years ago.

So *everybody* needs to go through the same steps to make sure their credit profile is as clean as possible when it comes time to pull the trigger on the biggest purchase that most of us will make in our lives. And the earlier you start on these steps, the less chance there'll be that you pay too much or lose out on an opportunity.

What are the stakes?

Even a small difference in your mortgage rate — a single point — means a payment more than $200 higher *per month* on that $350,000 home. For thirty years. The difference is even more dramatic if the loan is larger or the borrowing rate goes up.

There are plenty of legitimate reasons people don't qualify for the absolute best mortgage rate, but don't let it happen to you simply because of mistakes or other problems you could have easily addressed ahead of time.

That's just throwing good money away.

What Side of the Table Are You On?

I'm on your side, but it wasn't always that way.

For the first part of my career, I was a mortgage originator for Bank of America and then for Wells Fargo. My job was to sit on the other side of the table from average homebuyers like you and figure out two important details.

How could I get you approved for a mortgage? And how could I get you a mortgage "product" that benefitted me, e.g., it made *me* money?

Now, I wasn't some predator looking to push people into terrible loans with junk fees, high rates, and terrible terms. But there were plenty of originators who played that game.

But still, it's important for *everybody* to understand that the person on the other side of the table from you in the loan game — the mortgage originator or broker, the salesman at the car dealership, the credit card company, the bank holding the note behind your school loan —is *not on your side.* ✦✦✦✦✦✦✦

They might be nice and polite, and they might be trying to help you, but ultimately, they're looking out for themselves. They have bosses to answer to, guidelines to meet, bonuses to earn, and other problems to worry about.

When you walk into the mortgage originator's office, you have to understand that it's a negotiation, and you're responsible for taking care of yourself. That means coming in armed with as much information as you can about your own situation so that you can deal from a position of knowledge and strength.

But I can tell you that the vast, vast majority of people I saw as a mortgage originator — and the vast majority of the clients I end up seeing now — did not go into the home loan process with that in mind. Most people decide to buy a house, and they just sort of hope and pray that the mortgage person they heard about from a friend gets them a decent loan. And they go into the actual loan application process like one of those people on a daytime talk show who is waiting for the host to reveal the results of a mystery DNA test.

They know what they want to hear, and they kind of know what is probably coming, and now they're waiting to see where it all ends up.

I'm going to take away the mystery.

Let me describe for you what it's like to be on the other side of the table.

When you, the prospective homeowner, walk in, I might make small talk with you and chat about your family and your job, but the first and main thing I want to see is your credit score.

I'm going to learn a lot from how you respond to that question. Some common answers?

1. "I don't want to pull my credit, because it will hurt my score."
2. "We don't have to do that. I know it looks good."

3. "I have a great salary. It should be no problem to get a loan."

4. "I just bought it from one of those credit review websites. Can we use that report?"

My responses?

1. Not really.
2. Yes, we do.
3. Income matters, but it's evaluated down the line.
4. No, we can't.

No mortgage process is going to take even a baby step forward without a baseline examination of your credit report. And when I say credit report, I'm talking about the one we detailed in the second chapter — your official FICO score, as generated by information from one of the three credit bureaus. The score you show on that credit report is going to put you in a certain interest rate ballpark for loans you might be qualified to receive.

Once I have a general idea of what score you have, I'm going to go one level deeper and take a look at your credit profile. What kinds of accounts make up your score? Do you have a variety of credit sources, and have those accounts been open a long time? And then, only after I've looked at those factors, do I start to consider income — which will give me an idea of how much loan you can "afford."

One day, in my current life as a credit advisor, one of my good friends came to my office in a near-depression because he had been turned down for a conventional mortgage loan. His FICO score was 805 — which would normally qualify somebody for the very best rates and a loan that would sail right through. And he had an income healthy enough to support the loan he wanted to take out.

But even with that great FICO score, he had only one account open, and the bank originating the loan didn't like that. It was willing to underwrite the loan, but with an interest rate so egregiously high that my friend dismissed the idea out of hand.

85

Another client, a musician, came from Europe years ago. Thanks to a big hit a few decades ago, he had bought a huge house in California with cash. Now, he wanted to get a mortgage, but he had no real credit history in this country. He had millions of dollars in the bank, but, oddly, no credit score. He couldn't get a simple credit card, never mind a mortgage. That's a common problem for people who get transferred for business from a different country to the United States — or for professional athletes who just signed their first contract as twenty-year-olds.

By the Numbers

So what does this mean for you? Why do most people go into that first meeting with so little knowledge about what is about to happen?

Because the lack of consumer information works in the mortgage company's favor. If you don't know how you're being evaluated — if you're a great, good, average, or poor (whatever those terms mean) risk — you don't have any leverage in the transaction. It makes it harder for you to shop around for an interest rate, and in the end, you're probably going to pay a higher rate than you should.

US
Ave
680

Best
740

Let's revisit the numbers we talked about in Chapter 3, so you can see what I'm talking about.

The average FICO score in the United States is about 680. In general terms, a score above 740 is considered "tier 1," or the best. The middle tier (or tier 2) is from about 700 to 739, while below 700 is considered tier 3.

But in the world of home mortgages, the lowest number you're going to be able to get away with — and still qualify for some sort of loan — is 640, and that's for a buyer who gets an FHA-backed loan with private mortgage insurance and super-high rates.

If you're on the regular private mortgage market and you're not buying a first home, the lowest credit score you can have and still qualify is 660. And at that level, you're going to have an interest rate *almost 2 points higher* than somebody with pristine credit in the mid-700s.

Those 2 points in interest might not sound like much, but they make a huge difference in your monthly payment. And when you take that monthly payment and fold it into the general formula that mortgage originators use to determine how much you can afford — as a percent of your monthly income — it dramatically changes how much house you can afford to buy.

For example, a customer with pristine credit might qualify for a 5 percent loan. On a $300,000 house with a 20 percent down payment, that translates into a monthly payment of $1,288. At 6.25 percent, that same $240,000 loan translates into $1,478 a month. Property taxes usually range from about 1 to 2 percent of the home's value. We'll call it $4,500 for this exercise, which adds another $375 per month to each of those tabs — or $1,663 for the great-credit person and $1,853 for the person with mediocre credit.*

Banks like to see no more than 28 percent of your gross monthly income going to housing and taxes. That means the person with great credit is going to need to earn at least $57,500 to get the $240,000 loan. But the person who has mediocre credit? They will

*All of these discussions are about what are called "conforming" loans — loans less than $417,000 for most of the country. If you want to borrow more than that — either for a bigger house or because you're in a more expensive part of the country — there are different credit thresholds for those kinds of "jumbo" loans. In most cases, you'll need at least a 700 credit score to get a jumbo loan. In expensive parts of the country, like New York City and San Francisco, you can get a "jumbo conforming" loan with a 680 score, but you'll pay a higher interest rate than you would for a conforming loan.

have to earn almost $10,000 more per year to qualify for the loan — $67,200.

To put it another way, if you make $75,000 and have perfect credit, you can buy a house that costs about $330,000 with a 20 percent down payment. If you make the same money, have the 20 percent down payment, but have a credit score of only 660, you're going to be able to buy a house that costs about $280,000.

It should be obvious by now that credit scores are extremely important when it comes to your monthly mortgage payment. Here's another reason why.

Loan originators divide borrowers' scores into 20-point groupings. The minimum score to qualify for the loan is 660, and the folks in that 660–679 tier of scores are going to pay the maximum rate — about 1.75 percent more than the lowest rate. The people in the next tier, 680–699, are going to pay about a point more. When your score gets above 740, you're going to qualify for that best rate.

But guess what? Those point brackets are ironclad. Which means if you miss the next higher classification by even a single point — say, 739 vs. 740 — you're going to be stuck paying the less-advantageous interest rate.

Given what we've discussed about how various minor issues can hurt your score by 10 or 20 points, it is very, very easy to see how one simple mistake on your credit report can ding you to the tune of thousands of dollars over the life of a thirty-year loan.

Problem is, because the numbers in most mortgage transactions are so large and the lengths of the loans are so long, many people go to the table without any real grasp on what it all really means. To many, a quarter of a percent over thirty years just doesn't seem like a big deal.

But making careless mistakes during this process can be way more painful financially than keeping a credit card with a rate that's a little high or buying a car that's slightly more than you can really afford.

Here's how the conversation will play out: if you come into the mortgage process with a credit score in that 680–719 range, the mortgage originator is going to tell you that you qualify for a loan, but because of your "less than optimal scores," you will need to either pay an upfront fee — "pay points" — or you will pay a higher interest rate throughout the life of the loan.

Paying points basically means you're paying some of the interest of the loan ahead of time. It's a way for the bank to offload some of its risk by collecting some of its money ahead of time.

Using that $240,000 loan we talked about before as an example, you might run into this common scenario. You might have the opportunity to take a 4 percent interest rate on your loan and pay 1 point up front or take the loan at 5 percent with no points.

To buy that 1 point, you multiply the loan amount by 0.01. That equals $2,400 — which would be an upfront cost you'd have to pay at closing, right along with your down payment, taxes, and other fees.

Nobody wants to come up with extra cash at a time when cash

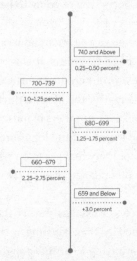

Loan Price Adjustment Based on Credit Score

is already hemorrhaging out the door, so the option to bake that point right into the loan becomes attractive, especially because it "only" changes the payment from $1,478 to $1,883. But here's the catch: over the life of the loan, the decision to avoid spending the $2,400 up front will end up costing you *more than $60,000* in extra interest paid.

Now, it might make sense for cash-flow purposes to pay the higher rate. But a vast majority of people go into these meetings totally focused on monthly payment and interest rate and never even consider the long-term ramifications of points. There's a big difference in outcomes, and you *do* have a choice. Make sure you're making an informed one.

You have to go through similar math when you consider your down payment. Many people don't have the 20 percent to put down, so they are required to pay something called private mortgage insurance (PMI). It's basically a surcharge that covers the lender in the event that you stop paying your mortgage when you don't have much equity in the home. It ranges from about .5 to 1 percent of the loan value, which can amount to hundreds of dollars per month. You have to figure out the long-term cost for paying that money — which you'll never get back — vs. securing the 20 percent down payment. Another important consideration is that many of the most attractive mortgage packages aren't available unless you have that 20 percent down, and that's *before* you get to paying the PMI. In effect, you'll be penalized *twice* — once with the PMI and a second time with a higher interest rate.

What to Do

If all this sounds discouraging, it certainly can be — especially if you aren't prepared. But if you plan ahead and take proactive steps to shore up potential problem areas, you can go into the mortgage process in the strongest possible position.

1. FIND OUT YOUR TRUE SCORE

I sound like a broken record by now, but it is imperative to know where you actually stand with the lender. This means getting a look at your genuine FICO score — *not* a pale substitute from FreeCred itReport.com or a credit "estimate" from sites like Credit Karma or Credit Sesame.

More than 40 percent of Americans have been victims of a data breach or identity theft, and many millions of those people have been offered "credit monitoring" because of it.

But the report you get from those monitoring services isn't the same as seeing your real FICO score. A site like Credit Karma gets its data from the credit bureaus, but it doesn't have access to the same FICO algorithms. Results from those kinds of sites tend to emphasize recent transactions highly, while your FICO score records seven years of credit history.

 To get the real thing, go at least 90 days before you start the mortgage process and make friends with one of the bankers at your local credit union. They'll often pull that report and let you see it. A talented real estate agent can also usually get you a copy. Banks and mortgage brokers want to maintain good relationships with agents so they get regular referrals, so they're almost always willing to provide that kind of information. (Why at least 90 days? Because when a lender pulls your score, they're locked into using that score for up to 90 days. If you find mistakes and fix them, you won't be able to have a new score considered for up to three months.)

If you're married and buying a house together, keep in mind that the lender will pool your income together, but will use the lower score from the two of you as the basis for qualifying you for a loan. It isn't a blended score. So if one spouse has a terrible score, applying for the mortgage in just one name is an option to consider.

When you get the report, it's imperative that you get one specifically pulled for a mortgage. The FICO models and algorithms change depending on what type of credit line you're trying to get, which means your score will change if you pull a mortgage report vs. one you'd get for a car loan. It's important to get a true representation of your situation.

2. ERASE SCORING MISTAKES

By the time you start shopping for a mortgage, it's too late to have mistakes in your credit file reported. When the mortgage originator pulls your credit and sees a remaining balance on a credit card that you've paid, but that fact hasn't shown up on your report yet, or an account listed as being in default by mistake, they're still bound to use that uncorrected report for up to 90 days, until a new one can be ordered. By that time, you might have lost the house you really wanted to another buyer.

The time to correct any mistakes is ahead of time. Get a copy of your credit report and go over it in detail. Make sure the account balances and open accounts you see are correct, and if they aren't, use the processes we described in Chapter 4 to get the problems erased from your report.

3. KEEP COLLECTIONS BURIED

If you do have old debts and collections on your report, it's not the end of the world. If you can work with the debtor and get those *erased* black marks *erased,* not just resolved, go ahead and pay those debts off. But if the debtor won't agree to remove the debt from your report as part of a resolution, ironically, you're far better off leaving it alone — especially if it's deep into the seven-year time frame your credit report covers.

Why?

Because any new activity on that debt moves it into fresher status within the bureaus' algorithms. A problem from six years ago figures much more lightly into the FICO algorithm than one from just last month. By paying toward it, yes, you're doing the "right" thing, but it will hurt your score in the short term to the tune of 70 to 100 points, right off the top. And if you're a person who never misses payments, a recently reported collection on an old debt is going to hurt you much more heavily than somebody who has a bunch of late payments on their record.

92

In other words, it's much easier to drop from 750 to 680 than it is to drop from 680 to 610.

4. MANAGE YOUR CREDIT ACCOUNTS

The single biggest factor in your credit score — 30 percent of it, in fact — is credit card debt. We've talked about it before, but the basics are worth going over again. *The closer you are to your credit limit on any individual card, the worse your score will be.* In almost every case, you will be better off using money you would otherwise have for a down payment to pay off your credit card debt. The difference in rate you'd receive for having 15 percent down vs. 20 is less than the penalty you get for having $20,000 in credit card debt against a $50,000 credit limit. In the very next chapter, we're going to go over exactly how you should be handling these accounts.

5. IMPROVE YOUR CREDIT SCORE PROFILE

Your credit score is the "title page" of your credit life, so to speak, but lenders are going to read the whole book. Ideally, you want to improve your credit score, but also improve the look of the numerous factors that go into the score.

The credit bureaus like to see a variety of different kinds of credit lines open — a mortgage, car loan, credit cards, and department store cards. They like to see that borrowers have all kinds of credit and that you do a good job paying all those kinds of bills. It's best to have four or five lines open, even if you don't use them all the time.

When you get just ahead of 60 days from having your credit pulled for your mortgage, you're going to want to both zero out your credit cards (if possible) and also refrain from using them as much as possible. Charge a few small items every month on a credit card and pay the bill on time, to show that you're regularly using it, but it's a good idea to avoid making big charges — even if you pay them off.

Zeroing out your balances every month is a great habit, but the credit bureaus don't necessarily receive information for your account in sync with when you're paying your creditors. You might charge $4,000 on your card for a new super-deluxe gas grill and pay it off at the end of the month — but if the creditor reported your account two days before you paid the bill, it looks like you have a $4,000 balance.

If you do need to make a big purchase and have the cash to do it, a debit card is the best choice. One useful component on Credit Karma's site is a "What If" estimator. It will let you punch in different variables for your credit accounts — things like balances — and get an estimate of how those variables will affect your score. It's great for a general look at pluses and minuses.

6. KNOW YOUR OPTIONS

When you get right down to it, shopping for a mortgage is like shopping for any other big-ticket item. You shouldn't be walking in cold and leaving yourself at the mercy of the mortgage broker or bank. The average person visits seven websites and spends more than three hours online doing research for a vacation. And they spend twice that much time researching a car purchase. It goes without saying you should be doing at least that much legwork when searching for a mortgage.

You want to shop around, and ideally you should have a person on your side who could give you some options. It used to be much easier to find a good mortgage broker. Any good real estate agent could give you a connection because it was in their interest to have potential clients qualified for loans.

But since the economic meltdown of 2008, the independent

mortgage brokerage business has been squished. The government added many extra hoops to the process to protect consumers, and it takes a full-time compliance person just to keep track of them. That pushed a lot of small mortgage shops out of business and left the big banks as the primary mortgage source.

Now, if you need a loan, you're probably going to start with the bank where you already do business. The good news is that all of the big banks are getting their money from the same place, so it's pretty easy to figure out what your mortgage rate *should* be, and their products are going to be similar. You definitely want to compare and contrast them, as well as compare those products to what a mortgage broker (if you can find one) tells you.

But before you get to that step, you have to have a conversation with yourself (and your significant other) about the parameters of the loan *ahead of time*. That means you don't go into the process with the house already picked out or the willingness to pay "whatever they approve us for."

You have to figure out what you can afford to pay in a down payment, then how much you can afford in a monthly payment, and then see what your credit scores are going to let you do. Know those parameters ahead of time, and then talk to the banks or brokers. If what you want to do and what the banks or brokers can give you lines up, then it's time to go shopping.

*

It may be a cliché, but knowledge is indeed power. If you can go to the mortgage table with the knowledge that your score and profile are as strong as possible *and* a general idea of what the mortgage broker is going to say, you're on much more equal footing. You're going to be able to ask questions and negotiate instead of just responding emotionally to information that surprised you.

You won't just have to take somebody's word for what's happening.

7

....

The Care and Feeding of Credit Cards

ONLY TWO INSTITUTIONS CAN LOAN you money and then change the interest rates they charge and the amount of the loan at will.

One of them is the Mafia.

The other one is a credit card company.

That might sound bizarre, but it's true. Credit card companies have more power than almost any other kind of organization within the world of consumer credit. And because they operate at the main intersection of so much of the American economy, they're a huge business, which means they have a ton of influence over how the rules are written regarding that business.

You do have some rights — and some leverage — when it comes to credit cards, but no other loan accounts you have in your entire portfolio are going to have interest rates as high as your credit cards, and no loan account you have will have more rules stacked against you.

Credit card companies can and do change the terms of your agreement, and it isn't usually in your favor. They're constantly monitoring your usage and credit scores to make sure you pay back the money you owe them — with interest.

The mortgage market is a larger one in terms of dollars, but trust me, nothing is more profitable than the credit card business. And having a credit card is basically required in the modern economy. As noted earlier, you're going to have a hard time buying an airline ticket, renting a car, booking a hotel room, or shopping online without one.

So hiding from the world of credit cards isn't going to work. If you don't have a credit card or you just want to make sure you have the best combination of interest rates and credit limits on the cards you do have, you're going to find the tools you need in this chapter. They've been reverse engineered from the credit card problems I've spent thousands of hours helping customers solve.

I want to start with the basics, because the vast majority of clients who come to see me don't know the most fundamental details of their credit card accounts — even after they've pulled their credit report.

*

Credit card companies put the most value on the clients they don't have yet. It's why most cards have a "teaser" rate that gives you a set amount of time at an artificially low interest rate if you transfer your balances from another credit card. The churn happens in two directions. Customers are always changing cards, and credit card companies are always poaching customers from other companies. (It also isn't any coincidence that credit card companies don't mind it that consumers are inadvertently hurting their credit scores when they don't develop a longer history with one particular account. If your scores are lower, you can be charged higher interest rates.)

But when the music stops — even temporarily — most people don't know what interest rate their new card resets to when the teaser rate expires. They don't really pay attention, and they just keep paying their monthly bill because whatever the rate is, it must be right.

Even if you're not somebody who changes cards often, you can fall into a complacency trap. You go along for a few years making your payments, and the rate on your card doesn't necessarily stay competitive with the market. But you don't have any specific complaints about the customer service with your credit card company, so a front-of-mind reason to change never presents itself. But even a 1 or 2 percentage point spread between your interest rate and the average rate for someone with your credit profile could mean hundreds of extra dollars in interest paid in a year if you're somebody who carries a balance.

Another reason many people get taken by surprise by their interest rates is because their borrowing profile changes over time. If you got a card many years ago during a time when you didn't carry any balances, the interest rate or credit line might not have been as important. But if you're now carrying balances on that same card, it might not be the right one for you anymore.

Why does this matter? Because about 40 percent of all credit cardholders carry a balance on at least one of their cards, and the average total of that balance is more than $15,000. That contrasts to the person who pays their balance every month, an average of $1,154.

Here's the point: if you're carrying $15,000 of credit card debt at 15 or 18 percent interest, you need a plan to manage that burden. And if you're one of the people who doesn't carry a balance, you want to make sure you have cards that match your goals.

Let's take a look at the average American credit cardholder. See if you recognize anything about that person. In 2015, Experian calculated that the average card carries a balance of $7,527. The average person has two cards, so another study's estimate of about $9,600 *per household* in credit card debt seems very reasonable. This translates into interest payments of more than $1,200 per year, at a time when interest rates have been historically low — and that doesn't even account for paying anything toward the principal balance.

The basic mechanics of a credit card are straightforward. When you use the card to pay for something, you get a bill at the end of the month. If you pay that bill in full, you don't owe any interest payments. But if you don't pay the full amount on the bill, you're charged daily interest on the balance you owe.

The card companies determine this based on the annual percentage rate (APR) on your card. An APR is slightly different than an interest rate in that the APR also includes any fees that go with the interest you pay. With a mortgage, the fees can be substantial, so an interest rate and APR are different things. But with credit cards, the fees are minimal, so for the sake of this conversation, we're going to call the APR and interest rate the same thing.

If you carry a balance, you'll get charged interest on that balance each day. Your interest total is determined by dividing your APR by 365, which results in a fractional number. Multiply your balance by that fraction and that is the amount added to your bill each day.

Let's put some real numbers to this so you can see it more clearly.

Say your card has a 15 percent APR. That translates into a daily rate of 0.041 percent. If you carry a balance of $1,000, 41 cents will be added to your balance on the first day of the billing cycle. On the second day, that new balance of $1,000.41 will be multiplied by 0.041, and that amount will get added on, and so on through the cycle. By the end of the month, your outstanding balance will be $1,013.

Credit card companies have rules for minimum payments — usually 1 to 3 percent of the total balance. If you pay just the minimum each month, the vast majority of your payment is going toward interest from the previous month, and it will take you years and years to pay off your bill. In fact, the credit card companies are required to show you, in each bill, how long it would take you to pay your bill if all you did was pay the minimum, as well as how much you'd pay in interest.

Let's take the average person, who is carrying $7,500 at 17 percent interest. With a minimum payment of $150 (or 2 percent), that person will need more than thirty years to pay off that debt and, along the way, will pay more than $23,500 in interest on a debt of $7,500.

It is obviously crucial to know exactly what interest rate you're paying on your credit cards, whether you carry a balance or not. As an informal survey, I always ask my new clients what rates they have on their cards before we compile a financial profile for them, just to see how close they can come to knowing them offhand. At least eight out of every ten people guess their rate to be something like 9 or 10 percent. In reality, it's always at least 15 percent and often more than 20 percent. If you were off by that much on your mortgage interest rate, your $1,600 monthly payment would turn into $2,230.

Yes, it's *that* big of a deal.

To give you some perspective, the average interest rate on all credit cards in the last thirty years has ranged from just under 13 percent (in 2003) to almost 19 percent (in 1985). If you're counting on those rates to head back toward where they were in 2003, you're probably going to be waiting a long time.

The rate on your credit cards is determined by a variety of factors. The first one is your credit score. If your score is 750 or higher, you're going to get the most competitive rates, and you're going to be able to aggressively shop between credit cards to get the best deal. The top-tier premium (not counting the ultra-premium cards like the American Express black card that celebrities and athletes carry) are ones like the American Express Platinum, the Chase Sapphire Reserve, and the Citi Prestige, all of which offer a variety of rewards and travel upgrades based on how much you spend.

In the middle tier, with a score of 700 or better, you'll be able to get a competitive gold card from one of those companies, with a healthy credit limit and an APR in the high teens. Below that, you're going to qualify for "basic" credit cards with relatively low limits or secured cards, which draw from cash you deposit into a connected account.

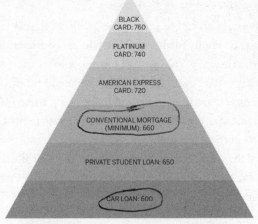

What Score Do You Need?

Once you're placed into a certain qualification bucket based on your credit score, your rate will be tied to the prime lending rate — the average rate at which the top commercial banks are lending to their best customers. Credit card companies base their rates on that rate and have a spread of around 12 percent between the prime rate and what their best customers pay. The spread obviously gets bigger if they think you're a bigger risk — but everybody's rate goes up when the prime rate increases. And starting in 2015, the prime rate began to rise again after having gone down continuously since 2006.

The third factor that affects your rates is the most challenging one because it's the only one that isn't transparent to you, the borrower. Each credit card company that issues you a card is doing what amounts to a two-year backward-look analysis of your spending and credit. It's monitoring every aspect of your credit report, along with how you use not only its credit card but all the other credit cards you own, too. It's watching how much you spend, how much you carry in balances, and how much you pay off in various cycles.

All of that information is constantly being crunched by various algorithms that are designed to predict how you'll behave over the *next* two years. If the algorithm predicts that you're going to be a worse credit risk, your interest rate will go up and your credit limit may go down. This is designed to do two things — to keep you from spending more money and to make sure the credit card company gets paid for what you do spend.

One call I get at least weekly comes from clients in a panic because their credit line was decreased, even though they made all their payments on time with that creditor. They want to know why, and I always tell them the same thing. It's a sign that that creditor has found something in the past two years that would indicate you're now more of a risk — a late payment, another card that's maxed out, or some other kind of ding that has showed up on your credit report. Any one of those reasons gives any of your credit card companies the ability to jack up your interest rate to the maximum amount — because they can. (If it happens to you, you need to review your credit report and see if there are any derogatory items reported or if there's been some kind of fraud.)

The algorithms are also insidious, because they predict how easy or hard it will be for you to go out and get a comparable credit card at comparable rates with a comparable credit line. If a card company can see that you are unlikely to be able to get another line like the one you currently have, it isn't going to worry very much about losing your business by raising your rate.

We've talked a lot throughout this book about the hit your credit scores can take when you miss payments, but credit card companies can hit you in other ways. For example, if you're 30 days past due, you're going to see a ding on your credit score. But if you miss a credit card payment by just *one* day, your credit card company can choose to hit you with a penalty interest rate.

It does depend on your credit score and how much the company values you as a customer, but it is extremely common for a regular 17 or 18 percent interest rate to get bumped to 29 percent as a penalty for a late payment. As a result, be sure to check the terms of your agreement to know how your company handles it, because their policies vary. It's actually a selling point for companies such as Discover, which markets the fact that it doesn't impose penalties for certain kinds of late payments as long as you bring the card's payments current in a certain amount of time.

I'm a fan of American Express for a variety of reasons — including how it gives cardholders unconditional protection for purchases made on the card — but one of my favorite things it does is the automatic review of your penalty rate after 45 days. If you're back current on your account, Amex will usually restore your previous rate automatically. It will even take the virtually-unheard-of-within-the-industry step of giving you back your card after you've defaulted — so long as you pay your balance in full. It'll also scrub your negative payment history. Those are powerful incentives for customers to resolve their issues quickly instead of making Amex chase them with a collection. In my experience, it's a good company.

If you do get hit with a late-payment fee and penalty rate, you can often call the credit card company and explain the circumstances and it'll back off — especially if you've been a good customer. Just make sure you ask for the right relief. Any credit card company will be happy to refund you a $25 late fee and continue to charge you 29 percent interest if the late fee is what you ask to be refunded. It's obviously way, way better to pay the fee as a signal that you're accepting responsibility for the mistake and ask for the interest rate to go back to what it was.

When the card company intends to change your rate, all it has to do is notify you at least 45 days ahead of the rate change. Yes, you have the right to protest the rate and close your account, but you'll have to pay off any balance you have or transfer it to a new card.

The credit card companies have a lot more room to maneuver than mortgage originators and student lenders, but President Barack Obama did sign into law a set of consumer protections in 2009 that gives you some leverage. It's called the Credit Card Accountability Responsibility and Disclosure (CARD) Act, and it has some important rules that every consumer should know.

It used to be that your credit card company could mail you statements whenever it wanted to, and it could change the due dates on your accounts at will. Those strategies were designed to essentially trick you into making a mistake that would lead to higher interest rates and penalty fees. If you were used to making a payment at a certain time or had the payments set to automatically disburse on a certain day through your bank's website, an off-cycle bill could mess that up without you even realizing it.

But the Credit CARD Act banned that activity, along with other sleazy tactics such as retroactively applying interest rate increases and slamming bad-credit secured-cardholders with huge fees just to get back into the credit market. It also gave people a way out of permanent penalty-interest purgatory. If you get hit with a penalty interest rate, the credit card companies are required to reset you to your original interest rate (or the current prevailing rate your credit score would qualify you for) if you make six consecutive on-time payments after the penalty. That now happens automatically, without you having to request reinstatement (but you should still check after six months to make sure).

The Credit CARD Act also made some behind-the-scenes improvements that make the credit card game more transparent and fair for everybody. Now, any payments you make to your credit card company go toward your highest-interest debt first. In addition, companies are no longer allowed to go to college campuses and recruit unsophisticated young borrowers with "trap cards" that come with some cheap freebies up front but crank up the interest rates for a group of people who are not very likely to have the money to pay.

Probably the most important rule to come out of CARD was that when you sign up for and are approved for a credit card, you're locked into that initial interest rate for a minimum of one year. That gives you a chance to get into a routine with the card and to fully understand what will happen to your rate in the long term. Of course, that doesn't absolve you from paying attention on month thirteen to make sure the terms of the credit card agreement aren't changing into something that doesn't work for you. Online services like Mint.com will actually monitor your credit card interest rates for you, which is a useful service if you don't mind sharing lots of personal financial information with a cloud-based company. You can even set it up to notify you by email or text when something changes. You'll get a note that tells you the change in rate, as well as the balance on the account in question. It makes monitoring your stuff a no-brainer.

The Anatomy of a Credit Card Spiral

If you're buried in credit card debt, this will all sound familiar to you. It tends to happen in just a few different ways. For some people, the problem comes along quickly, with one big crisis. The furnace breaks, and the only way to pay for it is with a credit card. A kid needs care in the emergency room, and a lot of it isn't covered by insurance. The only way to pay for it is with plastic.

For others, the issue grows slowly, year by year. Either they enjoy spending and don't think about the long-term consequences, or they're generally careful but just don't make enough money to balance their spending. The deficit grows slowly month by month until it's almost too big to handle.

Most people reach the tipping point when the minimum payments grow to where they almost can't pay them. And if all you can cover is the minimum payment, remember, you're looking at decades before you get clear — and that's only if you stop spending on the cards altogether.

When people get near this crisis point, the reflexive response by their credit card company tends to force their hand. If you miss a payment or two on one card and your limit gets reduced, other creditors will see your change in utilization percentage on your credit report — which has gone up because you now have a higher debt-to-limit ratio — and they will go ahead and change their interest rates and limits, too. They want to make sure they can collect something before you start thinking about exits like bankruptcy.

But those responses just make the downward spiral spin faster. You have smaller credit limits and way higher interest rates, and your minimum payments are getting bigger exactly at the time you're probably having a hard time paying them. Chase sees that you didn't pay Amex or that you were late on your car payment, and all of your creditors can jump on you for it. Their rationale is that they need to incentivize you to pay your bills and stop spending money.

When it gets to this point (or near it), it's understandable why many people make some bad decisions. They either give up and just stop paying on their credit cards, or they fall prey to one of the "credit counseling" companies we will talk about in Chapter 11.

The problem with either of those choices is that they both eventually lead to bankruptcy, and they both steal time that you could have been using to either dig yourself out of the hole or to start getting the bankruptcy over with. It doesn't make sense to throw up your hands and crater your credit score for a year by going delinquent or going through "credit counseling" — which craters your credit just as badly — only to *then* declare bankruptcy. You're just extending the pain for another year.

Whether you're getting close to that tipping point or not, it is absolutely crucial to pay attention if you start getting notifications about your credit lines being reduced or your interest rates going up. Those notices will make sense if you're going through some tough times, but they'll also be a warning if you can't think of any reason your financial situation has changed. In that case, it's almost always an indicator of a mistake or fraud on one of your credit reports, and you need to go get to the bottom of it.

Managing Your Credit Card Debt

The best protection is to recognize the credit card debt warning signs earlier, while you still have some options. Let's go back to the "average" cardholder, who has about $7,000 in debt on $20,000 of credit lines.

I'll take you through the exact process I use with my clients while we're sitting at my desk. It isn't the sexiest or most elegant, but it works. First, make a basic spreadsheet and create columns for the name of each credit card you own, interest rate, balance transfer rate, cash advance rate, and the current balance on the card.

As we've talked about, you'll often find that the credit card companies that treat you the best are the ones that are trying to poach your business. Now is the time to investigate just what other kinds of cards you could get and what the introductory offers are for those cards.

You can do this the old-fashioned way, by looking through a variety of bank websites and mailers and coming up with a list. One way to simplify the process is to go to Credit Karma's website. In exchange for giving it access to your credit score, it'll give you a tailored list of credit card offers for which you probably qualify. You then cross-shop for whatever options are the most important to you — introductory interest rate, airplane miles, annual fee, or whatever else.

If you identify a good new card to open, you can start juggling your balances from card to card, surfing from introductory rate to introductory rate. If you can get a new card with a $5,000 credit limit, you can move $5,000 from your highest interest cards over to the new one for the introductory period, which lasts for at least a year. You then have some time to pay down that total without losing so much of the payment to exorbitant interest.

One of my clients came in with a situation that was far more serious than just some financial hassles with a credit card company. She was in an abusive relationship, and she had to get out fast. She needed to find a new apartment, some furniture for it, and the retainer for her divorce lawyer. She had run up a credit card bill of more than $15,000, and she wasn't sure what to do.

But because she faced the issue early, her credit was still good enough that she had some options. She had the debt on two of her credit cards. We called them and found out that her rate was 15 percent on one and 19 percent on the other, and her cash advance interest rate was at a promotional rate of 8 percent for one year on her MasterCard. She also had $120,000 vested in her company 401(k), and her plan allowed her to borrow up to $20,000 from it.

Before I go any further, it's important to say up front that borrowing from your 401(k) has some real risks and disadvantages. Yes, the 401(k) money may be yours, but if you lose your job, take a new job, or simply quit, you're responsible for paying back the loan within 30 days of leaving your job, or you'll be hit with some serious penalties and taxes. You'll also be missing out on any potential stock market gains that money would have been a part of if it had stayed in the account.

That said, if you're in a stable job, you can use that balance as a kind of short-term bridge loan. Let me explain how it works. The vested cash in your 401(k) is yours but is only allowed to be taken out without penalty once you reach the age of fifty-nine and a half. But most plans allow you to borrow against that money, provided you pay it back within five years. You're charged interest on it, but you're paying the interest to yourself, back into the balance of your account. The loan also doesn't show up on your credit report, which makes it credit score neutral.

In my client's case, she was able to find a third credit card that offered her an introductory rate of zero percent for 18 months, with a credit line of $10,000. She transferred her balances to that card, and closed the newest of the two now-empty cards. But if she hadn't had good enough credit to find that new card, borrowing from her 401(k) would have been an option to consider.

By checking the spreadsheet you created, you can look for advantageous interest rates among your cards, like the 8 percent promotional cash advance rate my client had on one of her cards. If you were in that same position, you could take a 401(k) loan for $10,000, pay off all your credit card debt, and then use the cash advance offer to take $10,000 to pay back the 401(k) loan. The net effect would be that you move the debt from a 15-percent bucket to an 8-percent one for up to five years. Loans attached to most 401(k) plans don't have any prepayment penalties, which means you could pay extra toward the loan to retire it early.

Another less-than-conventional tool that is gaining popularity is peer-to-peer lending. A variety of companies are popping up that essentially sell into both sides of the loan transaction. They offer consumers a way to get access to money at a cheaper rate than a credit card, and they offer investors a way to achieve higher returns on their money. You can either go to them for a loan — which they vet just like a credit card company would, through your credit scores — or invest the cash that the company then uses to lend. Lending Club, Pave, and SoFi generally offer loan rates 5 or 6 points cheaper than a credit card, and the loan shows up on your credit report as an installment loan. It doesn't affect your score as negatively as a revolving debt does, and by using the funds to clear your credit card debt, your utilization percentage will look much better.

Whichever method you choose, just keep in mind what we've been talking about when it comes to your account's age. If you make some of these moves and zero out the balances on your cards, don't get hasty and cancel the ones that have a long positive history. You're going to hurt the length-of-credit component of your credit score. It's fine to surf from card to card, but try to confine your surfing to those cards that you haven't carried for very long, even if that means temporarily transferring the balance from a lower-rate card to a higher one while you look for another card with a low promotional rate.

Building Your Credit Game Plan

The best way to be prepared is to have an actual, physical game plan for your credit in the upcoming year. Your instinct is going to be to execute your plan around New Year's, but the credit card companies aren't dummies. They know most people are doing this at that time, so there aren't many consumer-friendly deals to be had. NerdWallet studied this exact subject and found that most of the best new customer programs are available at the time when the *fewest* customers are around looking for new deals. That means you should be doing your planning and hopping in the late summer and early fall.

Sit down and make up a rough sketch of where you want to be with your credit 365 days from now. Do you want to get a car loan? A mortgage? Improve your credit cards? Then you can make strategic decisions that keep this big picture in mind, but do it at a time when you aren't stressed out by being in the middle of a crisis.

When it comes to your credit cards, you want to plan for exactly what means the most to you — and do it before you need it. If you lose your job and need your credit cards to get by temporarily, you're not going to be able to go out and get those cards once the crisis has started. The perfect time to do it is when you're financially stable and showing low or no balances.

You might want a lower interest rate, a higher credit limit, or some airline or other retail rewards tied to what you spend on the card. Get out there and look around using the CreditKarma .com interface and by visiting some of the better forums. The users on CreditCards.com, MyFICO.com, and ThePointsGuy.com will have real-world anecdotes to share about almost any specific credit card issue you can imagine. Other users share what cards they've qualified to get with their credit scores, and they give first-person accounts of the relative value of the different benefits cards offer (and the quality of their customer service!). But as you shop, don't forget to examine what kind of options there are from the credit card companies you already have.

If you have a good credit score, call up your credit card issuer and ask what rates it has available or if it has any special offers coming up. Personally, I once carried a Capital One Platinum card, but I was looking to get into their Venture Rewards card because of the bonuses it offered for travel. By staying within the same credit card company family of Capital One, I didn't have to apply for a whole new credit card, and I was able to keep the value of a longer-life credit account on my report.

Your first stop when you look outside your current issuers should be the place where you do your regular banking. Check and see what kinds of cards it offers, and visit your branch in person to ask when it's going to be having specials or teaser rates to acquire new accounts. It's far more effective to do this in person because the employees you deal with there are often incentivized to sign up new accounts, and they'll be motivated to help put you in the right new product.

It is no exaggeration to say that two or three hours of attention and research into your credit card situation could pay you back with thousands and thousands of dollars in savings over the course of a year.

It's the best-paying part-time job you could ever find for yourself.

8

....

Protecting Your Credit Score from Identity Theft

PEOPLE TEND TO THINK OF identity theft the same way they view a car accident. It's something you know happens in real life, but it's unpleasant, so you try to put it out of your head. It's something that happens to other people. You'll worry about it when it happens to you.

It *is* happening to you.

Maybe not today or next week, but the days of identity theft being a rare problem are all but over. All you have to do is look at the news. Yahoo announced in late 2016 that more than one billion of its accounts had been compromised.

No big deal, right? After all, it's just email and fantasy football accounts. A minor nuisance.

Except that it isn't. Email hacks are the front line in identity theft and its relatives like credit card fraud because so much of our modern, technologically connected world works through email. Think about it. When you change a password to one of your online accounts, what happens? You get sent a confirmation email, which asks you to click and confirm you made the change.

If a hacker gains access to your email, it's like opening the front door to your entire financial ecosystem. They can use your information to open new lines of credit and also change passwords to other accounts — banks, credit cards, online merchants — and lock *you* out of your own life.

It's happening every day to millions and millions of people. They're getting their email and other accounts hacked, or their identities stolen the old-fashioned way — by having their credit cards duplicated, their mail stolen, or their Social Security number compromised and used in phony credit applications.

Not even the government is immune. Tens of thousands of folks are getting ripped off by tax return hackers every year through gaping loopholes in the e-filing system. If somebody knows your Social Security number, they can file a bogus return in your name, claiming a big refund. Long before the IRS figures out the game, the refund gets sent out to the crook. Your data has most likely been sold on to other bad guys to use to open phony credit accounts, too. And you're left to pick up the pieces.

We've all become so accustomed to the convenience of online shopping, seamless credit card transactions, and smartphones packed with all kinds of convenient (and vulnerable) information that we have inadvertently created a black-market buffet for criminals.

Think about who has access to your information. All you have to do is recount the dozens of forms you've filled out over the last few months. Do you do business with any of these folks or companies?

- Banks
- Credit card companies
- Stores
- Online merchants
- Doctors
- Employers
- Landlords

- Insurance companies
- Accountants
- Lawyers
- Schools

All of these entities have some or all of your personal information. And they may do a good job of protecting it. Or they might not. If a thief cracks one of those databases — or just gets access to an old file cabinet somewhere — they will have a wealth of information to either use or sell.

Visit the dark side of the web and you can buy bulk Social Security numbers from real victims for a few bucks apiece. A credit card number with the CVC security code costs about a dollar, while a set of duplicate health insurance credentials costs $20. Full identity "kitz" — Social Security number, account numbers, date of birth, addresses, and credit profile — cost about $1,200. With one of those, a crook can essentially duplicate your financial identity and take over as you, at least until you catch on. For the bad guys, they know exactly where to get these kitz. Just click, buy, and rip somebody off.

And why wouldn't they make a run for your data? If you compare the penalties for identity theft and other data crimes, they're minuscule in comparison to those for "hard" crimes like dealing drugs and selling weapons. Even "aggravated identity theft," which involves stealing somebody's identity for the purpose of creating false passports or citizenship papers, is only punishable by a minimum of two years in federal prison — at a comparatively "soft" prison. In contrast, possessing one hundred pot plants with the intent to sell illegally will get you a guaranteed five years of hard time.

Data criminals can steal and sell your information from the comfort of home — probably thousands of miles away from you — knowing it's very unlikely that they'll be caught or be in position to be charged in another jurisdiction. A cybercriminal in Prague isn't particularly worried about having to see a judge in Des Moines, Iowa.

In short, identity theft is very much a growth industry: it's easier, more lucrative, and less physically dangerous than other forms of crime. There is a direct correlation between the shrinking rate of street crime in the United States and the increase in information crimes. It's no shock that tens of thousands more criminals are trying it, and millions more consumers are becoming victims every year. The odds of getting caught are less than one in 1,000. Why pick up a knife or a gun when you have a laptop?

Even when you discover that identity theft is happening to you and are able to shut it down, the pain isn't over. It's just beginning, actually. Untangling that mess takes hours and hours of making calls, writing letters, cancelling accounts, and relentlessly following up for months and months to make sure the pieces are getting put back together.

The numbers are sobering. According to a Department of Justice study, almost twenty million people experience some kind of identity theft every year. That study is a few years old, so that number has certainly gone up. The same study said that the average victim lost $1,300 — which doesn't include the estimated two hundred hours it takes for the average case to be untangled. Total losses for all victims were $15 billion in 2014 and are estimated to be more than $20 billion in 2017 — and that doesn't count the total dollar value of the fraudulent transactions processed by various retailers and other organizations. That number could be as high as $250 billion. Annually.

Of course, it's far better to lock your information down to begin with and avoid all this pain. But even then, you could get compromised by the carelessness of one of those entities I described above. Or you might get scammed by a waiter with a card skimmer or by a person impersonating a bank representative on the phone.

In this chapter, I'm going to show you both how to play defense ahead of an identity breach and how to clean up the mess as quickly as possible if it does happen. We'll also go over how to freeze your credit so that nobody can access it without your express permission. Let's start by talking about how to identify the real risks in various areas of your life.

Financial Identity Theft

This is a book about your credit score, so it makes sense to start with the financial world. Your credit profile is essentially your financial passport. It shows where you've been and what kinds of places you'll be allowed to go.

As such, it isn't hard to understand why getting insider access to a credit profile — especially a pretty good one — is so attractive to a crook. If you can use a person's credit information to either gain access to a current line of credit or divert a completely new line, you have until that person discovers the theft to run up purchases and cash advances on that credit line.

For example, one client came to me with a fairly common situation. She had a credit card with a relatively high limit that she didn't use very often. One of the times she did use it was at a restaurant for a client dinner. Somebody at the restaurant had used a data skimmer to grab the information encoded in the black stripe on the back of the card. With a picture of the front and back of the card (hello, smartphone), a thief can make a facsimile of the real credit card and try to use it at places with less-than-perfect credit card security.

Since my client wasn't in the habit of using the card, she didn't keep track of the next bill — and she had set up automatic bill pay through her bank. But after two months, she opened the statement and got an incredibly unpleasant surprise. The thief had run up a $7,500 tab, and the automatic bill pay function had taken the $7,500 out of her checking account to pay for it.

The good news was that she wasn't stuck with having to untangle a series of delinquencies that she didn't cause. But the bad news was that it's much harder to deal with the credit card companies once they've already been paid. It took more than a week of work to get the problem sorted.

Credit cards aren't the only point of vulnerability. If a thief can crack your email account, they can cause a lot of problems. Your email address is pretty universally used as a username for online accounts. Once inside your email account, a thief can quickly see what other accounts you have. From there, he can either try the same password as your email account — upwards of 60 percent of people use the same password for multiple accounts, according to some studies — or just go around to the sites and request password resets. The confirmation emails come to the compromised address, and he's in business.

It's truly a terrible combination. The biggest email providers aren't terribly concerned about security or privacy, and it's a major vulnerability for the average person because so much hinges on that email account. Why bother hacking Bank of America or Chase through their very tight security when you can hack a Gmail or Yahoo account and get in through the unlocked side door? There's a reason why full email credentials cost $30 on the black market, while a Social Security number is just $3.

Another client was one of the people who had their Yahoo account information compromised. An identity thief used her login information — which was very similar to the login and password she used for Gmail, her main email account — to hack into her main email. From there, the thief gained access to her banking information and drained more than $10,000 from one of her accounts. It took her more than a month to work out the situation with the bank — and she was lucky. More and more banks are taking up to 90 days to resolve these claims, and during that period, you don't have access to your money. Can you live 90 days without cash?

Since the financial system relies on relatively straightforward data points like one's Social Security number and address to establish lines of credit, it isn't hard to see how a thief would try to establish new lines of credit using information they've gained from various sources.

For example, hundreds of colleges have been reporting that their alumni databases have been hacked over the last few years. They became rich targets because they didn't have much data security, and their records were filled with extremely valuable information — current addresses of alumni and data from when the students were enrolled at school. The most common way individual student numbers were assigned before the 2000s? Schools just used your Social Security number.

Which means that all a crook had to do was crack a low-security database to get pretty much everything they needed to try to create a bogus credit card account under your name. With just a little bit of care, the thief could create an account that would never even show up on your radar — until you saw the wreckage on your credit report months (or even years) later.

How? By establishing it under your credentials, but by using a different address. The card comes to a blind P.O. box, and the crook runs it up to the limit. At that point, they toss it and move on to the next victim. From your perspective, you never see a bill or get a notification that you're delinquent. Until you see your credit report.

Because there's so much information out in the digital world, that's become the easiest way for criminals to infiltrate your life. But it isn't the only way. Some old-fashioned techniques still work just fine.

One way to get somebody's personal information? By simply

asking for it. "Phishing" is the act of soliciting personal information from somebody via email, social media, or over the phone. The
thief will pose as your bank, looking for you to confirm the PIN on
your account via email or over the phone. Or somebody will email
to let you know that one of your online accounts has been compromised and will ask you to respond with your current password so
it can be reset.

It's easy to make fun of people who fall for the most obvious
phishing scams — like the folks who actually respond to the emails
from Nigeria or some other faraway country asking for a couple of
hundred dollars to release millions in some bogus financial settlement scam.

But many of the phishing scams out there now have become incredibly sophisticated. Crooks have the ability to create "spoof" or
"fake" emails that look as if they're really from your bank. They
have the right return email address and are formatted to look like
real correspondence. Plenty of sophisticated people have fallen for
phishing scams, so it's not something to take lightly.

How do you know if you're being phished?

First, be very guarded about sharing any sensitive information
over the phone or by email. You should only give out your Social
Security number within a transaction that you initiate, at the verified website of an organization that should need to have that information.

If you actually go to, say, BankofAmerica.com and try to
open a line of credit, it's OK to enter your Social Security number within the context of filling out an application. But if Bank
of America solicits you with an email offer for a certain kind of
card and gives you a link within the email, be very careful. It's
easy to be shifted off to a site that is designed only to suck in as
much of your personal information as possible so that you can be
ripped off.

Regarding phone calls: no reputable business is going to call you unsolicited and ask you for sensitive information like complete account numbers or a full Social Security number. It's why most business only use the last four digits of your Social as an ID — not the full number. If you get a call from somebody claiming to be from your bank or credit card company looking for that information, ask them for a name and phone number to call back, then check those with the company to see if they're legitimate.

Two other common low-tech ways thieves get access to sensitive identity information is through printed material. They either steal your mail from your mailbox or go through your trash to collect documents with identifying information like account numbers and Social Security numbers.

There's no way you can avoid getting mail with important information in it, but you can make your mail harder to steal by using a mailbox that locks or having the mail come through a slot that goes directly inside your house.

As far as what leaves your house, be sure to play closer attention to what you toss in the trash. I'm not suggesting you have to shred every document. I put all of my outgoing paperwork into a bin, and once a week, I sort through it to pull out pages with identifying information. Those pages get shredded, while the rest goes into the trash. Be sure to be extra careful with items like credit card solicitations. You want to either open those envelopes and make sure there's nothing useful to a thief inside or shred them before throwing them away. All it takes is for somebody to pick one of those envelopes out and fill it out in your name — but with a different address — to start some trouble.

*

Think of the information you could potentially share either over email or phone as the configuration of a stoplight. *Red light* information is stuff you should almost never share (and be very cautious if you do). *Yellow light* information is sensitive and requires some care. *Green light* information is generally OK to share.

Red
Full or partial Social Security number
Credit card number
Mother's maiden name

Yellow
CVC number
Date of birth
Cell phone number
High school mascot

Green
Name
Address

Medical Identity Theft

Credit card balances, student debt, mortgage payments, and car loans cause people plenty of stress, but at least those financial tools — and the statements that come with them — are relatively straightforward.

The world of medical treatment is extremely confusing and that's even if you have insurance. It's always a struggle to figure out what's covered and what isn't, how things are being paid for, and what happens when a bill doesn't get paid. The layers and layers of bureaucracy between the consumer, the hospital, and the insurance company leave plenty of space for mistakes to be made — and for crooks to try to get involved.

And because most people don't come into month-to-month contact with their health insurance the way they do with a credit card or mortgage statement, they aren't sure what to look for when it comes to mistakes or fraud.

So it shouldn't be a huge surprise that medical identity theft is one of the fastest growing forms of information crime in the United States. You might be wondering what motivation a bad guy would have to hijack your medical information and why I'm even talking about it in a book about credit scores.

I'll answer the second question first. Medical debt is one of the main reasons consumers get a negative hit from one of the credit bureaus. Often, it's because a relatively small medical debt gets missed over the course of insurance covering most of a procedure, and the consumer doesn't know about the oversight. By the time it gets noticed, that relatively small debt has crushed the consumer's credit score. In other cases, the sheer size of an uncovered medical expense can drive a consumer straight to bankruptcy. In fact, more than 60 percent of all bankruptcies are related to medical debt. In other words, the financial and medical worlds are directly related.

As for criminal motivation, there's plenty. With access to your medical credentials — like insurance group ID numbers, Social Security number, or Medicare number — a bad guy can cause you a variety of problems. He can use your credentials to see a doctor and get bogus prescription drugs, which are then sold on the black market. Or, if he has some knowledge of medical billing procedures, he can sell the information to dirty medical clinics that run up gigantic phony medical bills and hit your insurance company for payment. By the time anybody sorts out what has been going on, the crooks have already closed up shop and moved along — with the insurance company's money. You're left with uncovered medical expenses on your tab that you don't know anything about and the task of sorting it all out.

Doing that legwork to untangle the mess might be a headache, but the physical problems that medical identity theft creates can be even more serious. It only takes a keystroke error from an insurance company to intermingle your legitimate medical records with bogus ones set up by the bad guy. That leaves a paper trail that could be misinterpreted by your doctor or the insurance company and cause you to either be denied coverage you should be getting or get treatment for a problem you don't necessarily have. Those could be life-and-death mistakes.

This is why you have to be as vigilant with your medical information as you are with your financial information. Treat those ID cards (and your Social Security card) just like a credit card, because in many ways they work the same. In fact, you should resist giving your Social Security number to the hospital because there's no legal requirement to do so, and the hospital will only be using it to sell your medical debt to a collector if you run into a problem later on. Plus, hospitals have proven to be some of the easiest organizations for hackers to penetrate.

The tools for handling your medical information are very similar to those that you use to handle your financial life. You have to pay attention to *all* the correspondence that comes from your insurance company. Make sure the bills and claims of service match with services you've actually used and procedures you've had. For example, if you get a letter saying a certain kind of service hasn't been preapproved — and you've never tried to get that particular kind of service — that's an indication somebody might be trying to access your account.

For some people, this kind of attention is going to be a big job. If you have a lot of medical problems or a big family with a lot of people who receive medical treatment, you're going to have to juggle a lot of balls. Being very careful and attentive about reading your credit report is another way you can keep on top of this information.

Here's the bottom line: if medical collections you don't recognize are appearing on your credit report, it's imperative that you track those collections to their root, before the problem gets bigger.

Child Identity Theft

Kids have two things that make them very attractive to identity thieves. They have Social Security numbers, and they have a clean financial slate. If a thief can get a kid's Social, they can set up bogus accounts under that name and number and rely on the fact that a kid isn't in a position to be monitoring their credit report — or complain if they don't get approved for a loan.

The bureaus' official policies are that they don't compile credit records for anybody under eighteen years old. But if a child's data is compromised and used to create a phony profile — a legitimate name and Social Security number, but a fake birth date — it's something the child might not discover until they turn eighteen and try to apply for a credit account for real. Then they're in for a rude surprise. One of the most famous cases is that of a nineteen-year-old woman who applied for a credit card when she was in college. She discovered that identity thieves had taken over when she was nine and had run up more than $1 million in debts.

If you suspect child identity theft has happened, call the three main credit bureaus to notify them and ask if they have any record of credit being opened in that name. You'll be asked to provide the name and Social. The answer you want to hear is that they have no records found under those credentials. You can also request that the credit profile be frozen until age eighteen.

Not all of the violations come at the hands of the criminals, either. Because of the prevalence of social media, kids are sharing way, way more information with the world than ever before. They're doing everything online — including unknowingly giving information to people who will use it to hurt them or you.

Need an example? When a kid posts a picture of his or her parents partying at a vacation spot in the Bahamas, it isn't hard to figure out that people aren't home guarding the house. One client's son tweeted that he and his parents were about to board a flight from China back home to California. By the time they got off the plane in Los Angeles, a thief had wired all of the money out of one of their accounts.

Guarding Your Identity

If all of this sounds pretty dire, it should. It's a serious issue, and you need to take aggressive steps, both to prevent it from happening to you and to fix it if does. It starts with adapting your behavior to reflect some of these risks.

I'll give you the same speech I give my high-profile and entertainment and sports clients. Information you share willingly with the world — either in the form of email, subscription data with an online service, or even what you put out through social media like Facebook and Twitter — is all fair game for data thieves. If they target you, they're going to use everything at their disposal.

Giving out some information is unavoidable. But you can control a lot of it yourself. It's obviously unwise to broadcast your Social Security number, but you need to be careful with other kinds of information as well, to avoid giving data thieves clues they can use to find your information and make guesses about things like passwords.

On social media, avoid giving out specific details, like your address, children's names, birth date, or phone number. Even seemingly innocuous information like a phone number can be used by a thief to verify information with a rookie phone representative and get a foot in the door. You've done the drill enough times yourself when talking to, say, a representative from your cell phone provider. Any kind of identifying information they're asking you to confirm your identity isn't information you should be making easy for somebody to find online.

If you need proof that putting more information out there is dangerous, let me take you to the fifth-grade class at Saint Elizabeth Catholic Academy in Queens, New York. I asked thirty ten-year-olds to use the internet to see what kind of information they could find about their favorite celebrities. It took one kid just twenty-one minutes to come up with enough information from web searches to be able to open a line of credit in that celebrity's name. Hard to believe, but absolutely true.

Your computer and smartphone are two of the most useful pieces of equipment you own, but they can both get you into serious trouble if you aren't careful.

On your computer, the web browser is the information superhighway thieves use to get in — and take your data out. Most people don't even take the most basic steps to secure themselves, like using secure passwords and being careful about how they log in and out of various financial websites.

Some basic rules of the road:

- Use two-factor authentication for your email accounts. Most email providers offer it, and it's a simple way to block unauthorized access. It requires two pieces of information from you to enter the account or change information — a password and a second form of authentication through a different device, like a text message to your phone.
- Make your passwords different for each site, and make them something nobody could easily guess. Something with a mixture of letters, numbers, and symbols is obviously going to be better than simple phrases. Even better are the password managers that generate random passwords for every site you use. You control them with a single master password only you know.
- Keep an up-to-date version of anti-virus software on your machine at all times, and update your browser regularly to make sure its security patches are in place.

- When you log in to a bank, credit card, or other sensitive financial website, make sure you're doing it on a trusted network at home or work, not a public one at a library or a coffee shop. It's extremely easy for a hacker to snoop on public Wi-Fi traffic and snag your information.
- No matter what network you use, be sure to quit out of your browser completely after you log out of your financial websites. Otherwise, your data could be stored.
- Before you get rid of your computer, be sure to erase the hard drive completely with reputable software. If you just trash your files, a thief can easily resurrect them.

  Smartphones carry just as much important information — especially now that they're being used as digital wallets for checkout at your favorite supermarket. Your phone is filled with information that a data thief could use to steal your identity or appropriate one of your financial accounts. You need to treat it just as you would your personal computer.

- At the minimum, use a PIN to secure your phone. Virtually every phone has a feature that disables the phone if somebody punches in the wrong PIN repeatedly. Use this feature, even if it might be annoying to constantly be typing in a PIN. The biometric fingerprint readers on iPhones are great for convenience and perform the same function.
- Remember that access into your phone is like gaining access into your email account. If a hacker can read your email, they can gain entry to a lot of your financial world. Consider creating a specific email address just for your most sensitive financial accounts and keeping that account separate from the built-in mail apps on your phone. If you need access, you can always go to the phone's web browser and log in that way.
- Speaking of browsers, treat the browser on your phone like the one on your computer. Be cautious about the mobile

Wi-Fi networks you use, and quit out of the phone browser after you've used it to log into a financial account.

- Public Wi-Fi isn't secure. You're better off using your cell signal to log into your financial apps. It's much more difficult for a hacker to intercept information traveling on a cell signal than a public Wi-Fi network.

Be Careful About Credit Monitoring

Credit cards require some common sense, like not spreading your number, expiration date, and authentication code around indiscriminately. Some not-so-obvious care needs to be taken when you're out in the world, too. If you're going someplace where your credit card is going to be swiped when out of your possession and view — like at a restaurant — make sure you are in fact using a credit card and not a debit card. If your card should happen to be skimmed and duplicated, a credit card has built-in consumer protections that a debit card doesn't. The checking or savings account attached to your debit card could be cleaned out by the time you finish your dinner and make it home.

A comprehensive defense plan means you have to be a watchdog, too. You're adding surveillance, so to speak. That means keeping track of what's on your credit report and knowing when new activity on your report takes place.

If you've been a victim of one of the famous data breaches the last few years — like the ones with Yahoo, Target, or Home Depot — you probably got a letter or email from one of those companies offering you free credit monitoring as an apology for failing to protect your data. It's a service that normally costs about $10 a month if you bought it on your own.

Credit monitoring is supposed to do just what it sounds like

—monitor your credit and inform you of any suspicious changes. That might sound like a good idea and a way to get some peace of mind. The idea that somebody is looking out for your score even when you aren't is certainly comforting.

Except that isn't what's happening.

Credit monitoring works fine in some limited cases. If you have one of the better services that monitors all three bureaus (the free services will usually only monitor one of the three), it will tell you when a new credit inquiry has hit your credit report. If you went to the car dealership and applied for a loan to get a car, it would make sense that you'd get a notification that the dealership ran your credit. But if you got a notification about an inquiry from Bank of America for a new credit card and you didn't apply for one, you'd have a reason to do some more digging.

But the problem is that credit monitoring offers a very false sense of security. For example, credit monitoring usually doesn't keep track of fraudulent credit card activity on accounts you've already opened. And it doesn't track fraudulent activity that happens outside very specific parameters. If somebody uses your Social Security number, but with a different name or address, you won't be notified. You also won't hear about it if somebody uses your identity and Social Security number to sign up for a cell phone or cable service.

The services that most credit monitoring provides aren't any different than ones you could handle yourself by monitoring your own credit through the process I'm going to describe below. And by doing it yourself—and keeping track of *all* the ways crooks can get into your business—you're going to have real peace of mind.

If you've read this far, you already know that you need to be getting copies of your credit report from the three bureaus every year. That will give you a good overall picture of your credit position, but if you get the reports at the exact same time, you're not going to see potential fraud. Buy a cheap desktop calendar, and mark down some important dates.

Ask for your free credit report from each of the three bureaus, but stagger the dates so that you're doing it from one of the three bureaus every four months. That will give you a good level of preliminary indication if something is wrong — and give you a good vantage point to see if any accounts from other kinds of creditors, like cell phone or cable companies, have been opened.

Now, you need a plan to organize and review the information that comes into your house. When you get a credit card bill — either in the mail or online — you need to review it carefully and make sure each of the charges is legitimate. As we talked about in the medical fraud section, you need to do the same with your insurance statements. Create a central storage place for these documents — and the original cards, like your insurance card, Social Security card, and other identification papers — and a list of all your credit accounts and the corresponding account numbers and contact telephone numbers. Then you'll be able to quickly go down the list and take action if you lose your wallet or run into some other kind of issue.

In the same file, keep control of your important physical data — receipts, tax returns, and statements for your credit card, mortgage, car loan, and student loan — anything that has identifying information on it. Talk to your accountant or tax person about how long you need to save things, but make sure that you keep them in a centralized place with some security. I like to use a locked two-drawer file cabinet, hidden in the mechanical room in my basement. It has to be somewhere you can easily access, but not an obvious place where somebody who breaks in is going to look.

One of the benefits of online banking, credit card, and loan management is that it gives you a way to check in on your accounts in real time. And many of those companies even let you make your own reports detailing specific periods of time. You can lump similar expenses together or look at a bigger or smaller picture. You can treat it almost like an old-fashioned checkbook — matching receipts you keep in your wallet or purse with transactions on your cards. Anything you can do to keep a more regular eye on your situation is going to help.

What to Do When It Happens to You

Unfortunately, even if you do everything right, you could still be victimized, because there are still plenty of organizations out there that aren't as careful with your data as you would be. Or it could simply be a case where you've lost your wallet or had your purse stolen from the trunk of your car. That's the reality of the world we live in, but it doesn't have to blow a permanent hole in your credit report.

Like many medical conditions, the more time that passes before you get a diagnosis and begin treatment for identity theft, the more painful and substantial the treatment can be. If it does happen and you address it quickly, you can often reduce the pain and fix it in less time and for less hassle.

Say you've found that an unauthorized account has been opened. Or you've been notified that one of the companies you do business with has been breached, and hackers have all of your information. What do you do first?

The first step is to put a specific fraud alert on your credit file with each of the three bureaus. This requires them to notify you if anyone requests to see your credit or if an attempt is made to open a new credit account in your name.

You only have to request this from one of the individual bureaus, and they're required to notify the other two, but you must renew this request every 90 days. You can find the contact information for each bureau and where to call on my website, www.anthonymdav

enport.com/yourscore. (If you've already been a victim of identity theft and have filed a report with the FTC, which we'll cover below, you can put an extended fraud alert on your account for seven years without having to renew it. Active members of the military can also get a ten-year fraud alert put in place.)

Go through all of your reports from all three bureaus to identify *any* kind of unauthorized activity. Hackers will often open a small and hopefully unnoticeable account and test it out to see if the victim notices what's going on. Your job is to go through and identify any accounts you didn't open, inquiries you didn't authorize, and balances and debts you don't recognize. You also need to go through and make sure there are no variations of your name, address, and Social Security number on the report.

If you see an address you don't recognize, it could be the result of an honest mistake — or it could be evidence that a hacker put new information into your report. When the credit line was opened, the different address could have been the one the crook used to forward the credit cards and statements just so that you didn't notice what was going on.

Keep detailed notes on any discrepancies you find, and bring the information to your local police precinct to file a report. That report establishes the baseline for what has happened — and is something you're probably going to need to give to your creditors later on. When you get to the precinct, they're going to ask you a series of basic questions about what happened and to provide a statement of the facts. You'll also probably be asked for a copy of the account numbers and the credit report that shows the infiltration.

Resist the temptation to believe that the police are going to go out and immediately start beating the bushes to find the person who hacked you. They almost never do — and it's almost never somebody nearby who did it. What you're doing is simply establishing a record and proving to the creditors and bureaus that you jumped through the right hoops.

Once you've found the compromised accounts, call those creditors and ask to speak to their fraud department. Tell them you have reason to suspect identity theft, and ask them to close or freeze the affected accounts. Different companies might have slightly different policies and timelines for how to do this, but they all have to follow the law — and they have to freeze the accounts at your request. Let each creditor know you'll be sending (in writing) requests for applications and records pertaining to those accounts, and ask what documentation and forms they will need from you — and where to send them.

If it's your bank that has been affected, go to a branch in person and request to speak to a fraud specialist. Tell them about the breach, and request that all of your accounts — checking, savings, credit cards — be assigned different account numbers or closed. This is *extremely important* in a world where so many accounts are connected to each other digitally. Crooks will quickly try to transfer cash between your accounts, and your checking and savings could be drained before you even notice. That's a bigger headache to deal with in comparison to a credit card dispute, because credit card companies have very specific rules in place about disputes that are built in your favor. It's harder — and takes longer — to get cash restored to checking, savings, and debit card accounts, so it is crucial that you act on those issues very quickly.

Next, go to the identity theft website for the Federal Trade Commission, IdentityTheft.gov, and fill out the online Identity Theft Report form. This will create a specific file you can print out and use in conjunction with your police report to prove to creditors that you've been victimized.

From the time you file your paperwork with the FTC and your creditors, it usually takes about 60 days for the compromised accounts to be deleted from your credit report. That's obviously something you have to continuously monitor.

How to Freeze Your Credit

Once the affected accounts have been frozen or cancelled and you've created new, legitimate accounts, you can activate the one tool that can almost guarantee you won't experience identity theft in the future. In fact, you might want to use this tool even if you haven't been victimized.

I first learned about credit freezing when I was talking to a colleague about a series of high-profile entertainers who had been the victims of identity theft. The thieves had secured the complete identity credentials of a bunch of famous people, including many members of President Obama's cabinet.

As a result, there were plenty of conference calls among representatives of these famous people, the FBI, the White House, and the legal and security departments of the credit bureaus. The representatives of one of the celebrities involved asked me to help untangle the issues their client faced. As they described what had happened, a question popped into my head.

Why hadn't President Obama's identity been compromised?

Simple, said the folks from the entertainer's office. The president had a complete credit freeze on his account.

In a freeze, nobody can even inquire about your credit without your direct, authorized permission through the use of a secret PIN. Nobody will be able to open an account in your name because nobody will be able to see your credit information and make a decision about it. It can certainly make some day-to-day activities more clunky to accomplish — because the freeze has to be specifically lifted for you to, say, get a car insurance quote. But there's no more effective way to lock down your information so that only those people you authorize can see it. It's very different than a fraud alert, which only tells you about activity as it goes on. The freeze stops things from happening before they start.

Obviously, the credit bureaus aren't super excited for you to be able to do this because they're in the business of doing business. They (and the credit card companies) accept a certain amount of inevitable credit card fraud as the price of making transactions go through quickly and smoothly.

But the rules are in place for you to do it, provided you follow these specific steps.

First, use the numbers and websites on my website (www .anthonymdavenport.com/yourscore) to contact each credit bureau separately to request the credit freeze. You'll be required to give your name, Social, address, and date of birth, and pay a nominal fee ($10 per bureau, sometimes free if you've already been the victim of identity theft). Once you register, you'll get a letter in the mail from each bureau with a PIN. If you ever want to lift the freeze — say, to apply for a mortgage — you need to call each bureau and use the PIN to give access to your credit, which will be provided within three days. You can either provide access to a specific creditor or open your account to anybody for a specific period of time. Lifting the freeze also costs $10 for each bureau.

To re-freeze your account afterward, you'll have to go through the process again with all three bureaus and pay the fee again. It's designed to be a headache, but an hour of effort each time you have to do it will give you the ultimate peace of mind.

The Aftermath

After you've sorted out the affected accounts, it's important to go back to each creditor and request a letter from them that recounts the basic facts — that your account was fraudulently opened or tampered with and that it has been closed. That documentation will help down the line if you have a dispute with one of the credit bureaus about something that is appearing on your credit report when it shouldn't.

You should also consider removing yourself from the national databases that marketers use to send you unsolicited offers for things like credit cards. To opt out of mailings, go to DMAChoice .com and fill out the online form. You can do the same for tele-marketing by going to the Federal Trade Commission's registry at donotcall.gov.

Most of all, don't get discouraged. Identity theft can be scary and demoralizing, but even the worst cases can be turned around with some knowledge and persistence.

Remember that incident I described where the celebrities had their identities compromised while the president's stayed locked down? The celebrity in question had one of the worst cases of identity theft I've ever seen.

His Social Security card and driver's license were circulating on the internet, and his credit report had become so filled with bogus accounts and fraud that the bureaus took the almost unprecedented step of pulling his report from the system entirely. He was actually reassigned a new Social Security number — something that usually only happens to people in the Witness Protection Program.

After he received the new Social, my job was to figure out how to re-create his credit profile to represent what it was before the hacks started. I had to go through and eliminate the bogus accounts on the old Social and have the legitimate ones transferred to the new number, while putting the safeguards we've been talking about in this chapter into place.

With a security freeze and fraud alert in place on his new Social, the client was able to re-establish his credit, and after about two months, his credit score was back up near 800.

If that problem can be solved, so can yours.

9

....

The "Newbie": Establishing Credit for the First Time

I'M NOT THAT OLD, and I didn't go to college all that long ago. But it was a different financial world in the 1990s. Credit card companies were doing all they could to bring young people into the game back then, offering low-interest cards to pretty much anybody who walked by the table at their college's student union. It was a credit feeding frenzy to find new clients, and almost every credit card company was a part of it.

It isn't that way anymore. Ever since the financial crisis that started in 2007, credit has become way harder to get. And that's true all the way up and down the spectrum — from $500-limit credit cards for twenty-year-olds to $250,000 mortgage loans for young couples. In fact, credit card companies aren't even allowed to solicit on college campuses anymore.

Now, everybody from Capital One to Bank of America wants to take a look at that credit profile. And if you're twenty-five years old or younger, you most likely have either a nonexistent credit profile or one that's pretty one-dimensional. Maybe you have four years of school debt you haven't started paying back yet.

The numbers in dozens of studies on credit show it, too. Young people twenty-five and under are initiating new lines of credit at a lower rate than any time since the 1930s, both because credit is harder to get and because they're already strapped by those big school loan payments and low starting salaries.

Now, if you want to enter the world of consumer credit — as a young person, or even as somebody over twenty-five who is coming to the United States to work from somewhere else in the world — you need to have a plan. You're going to have to do more than just sign your name and pick up your free T-shirt.

I shouldn't even phrase it as "want to." When you have student loans to manage, the workplace to enter, car loans to qualify for, rental apartments and home mortgages to get, and insurance to set up, you *have* to be a part of the world of credit. And that covers just about everybody in the modern American world.

There are some prominent people in the world of personal finance, such as Dave Ramsey, who believe your goal should be to have "credit score zero" — meaning you don't borrow money and you don't participate in the consumer credit marketplace. Under that scenario, you'd never apply for a line of credit and the credit bureaus wouldn't have a score for you. Dave brags on his show about having no credit score himself. Now, in fairness, I do see where he's coming from. His goal is to convince people to avoid racking up a bunch of debt — and that part is good advice.

But as we talked about in the second chapter, you're going to be evaluated through your credit score for a lot more than just credit cards and mortgages. If you totally opt out of the system, you're going to restrict your options. That's something Dave doesn't have to worry about as the owner of a company with five hundred employees and real estate that he can pay for with cash. As a regular person, you might be able to find a credit union that will manually underwrite you for a mortgage. But the truth is, you won't get the loan if you don't get the job — the job where employers use a credit check as a pre-interview screen.

It might be strange to think about a multimillionaire twenty-year-old professional athlete or a world-famous musician from Europe being in the same boat as the kid who is just walking out of college with a marketing degree and a beginner job, but that really is the case.

As noted in Chapter 2, it doesn't matter what income you have, what hit singles you've written, or what round you were drafted. Your credit score is based on your history of *using* credit. So, if you haven't used credit in this country, you aren't going to have a score.

Here's the point: if you're coming out of school with a stack of student loans that have, up to this point, been deferred, you don't have any positive credit history — just debt. Or if you lived overseas and have come to the United States on a work permit, you're not going to be able to get an American credit card without getting a Social Security number — and you aren't going to have a credit score until you do that. Whatever positive credit you built up in your home country doesn't transfer to the United States.

Let me give you an extreme example: if you played one season of college basketball, turned pro, and were picked in the first round of the NBA draft, you're going to have millions from your signing bonus and major shoe endorsement money in your bank account. But unless you've interacted with the world of credit, those millions won't translate into any kind of credit score.

One of my clients fit that exact scenario a couple of years ago. He was twenty years old, and after playing a year of college ball, he was drafted very high. After signing his contract and his shoe deal, he had just under $3 million in cash in his bank account. He went out and bought himself a new car, but when he tried to insure it, he couldn't find a company that would give him a policy.

His manager called me to see if I could help straighten out the problem. We started by pulling his credit from each of the three bureaus. According to two of them, he didn't have any score. He was basically a nonentity. With the third, he had a score, but it was in the 500s. Back in high school, he had been hit with a medical collection for a copay he had through his mother's insurance. He didn't know anything about it, and it had followed him for four years. The total of the bill that was chasing him and keeping his credit score down? About $100.

Another set of clients came to me after they had relocated from Hong Kong, where they ran a very successful software business. A married couple, they were in the process of relocating to New York City to expand their business into North America. They had a lot of cash, but were interested in financing a home purchase because of how low the interest rates were on mortgages.

If they were financing a condo in Hong Kong, they would have had plenty of choices. But since their credit history was overseas and they were relocating to live in a New York City building, they discovered that they would need to use the American credit system to qualify for their mortgage. Just like the basketball player, the amount of money they had in the bank didn't make any difference to the credit bureaus — and it didn't even get them any brownie points with an American bank because they had kept their cash with the Bank of China.

A country music star's manager came to me because her client was having trouble getting even basic credit. The manager had been booking hotel rooms for her client under her own personal credit card, but, as it turned out, the music star wasn't able to rent a car because she didn't have her own credit card. She couldn't do something as seemingly simple as buy a plane ticket on her own.

Before she hit it big, the singer had spent five years waiting tables in Nashville, living paycheck to paycheck. She shared a small apartment with a friend and had an old car her parents had given her when she graduated from high school. She had never developed a credit profile, and that was still true after two years of sold-out concerts and top-selling singles on iTunes. Hard to believe, but the computer-automated systems that the credit card companies use didn't care that the singer had performed at the Grammys and was about to headline a national tour. In terms of her credit, she didn't really exist.

One client came to me because he was trying to get a mortgage on an $800,000 apartment in New York City. He was a vice president of one of the major media companies, and he had used corporate credit cards, took corporate car service to get around, and rented the same small apartment for virtually all of his credit life — more than twenty years. He made $500,000 per year, had virtually no expenses, and was prepared to put down a big down payment. But for the bank's purposes, he was an unknown.

For each one of those clients, they had to start the credit process in the same way a new college graduate would after taking a regular job in a regular town anywhere in the United States. It's like learning to walk. Every kid has to go through it and figure it out before they can start to run.

What follows is the exact game plan I use with my new credit clients, divided into two paths. The first route is what I call the "slam path." If you come to me and you need a credit score in the 700s in 90 days, this is the path you take. It requires a lot of time and attention, as well as the help of some understanding friends or family members who would be willing to let you tag along on their good credit temporarily.

The second route is the "conventional path," for people who don't have access to a willing friend or family member who has established credit. It's totally doable for anybody who doesn't have a footprint with the credit bureaus, and it can get you in the 700s and qualified for a top-tier mortgage in nine months to a year. If you're a young person taking this route, it would be worth it to start doing this *before* you graduate, so you're ready to hit the work world at full speed.

The 90-Day Credit Slam

To get on the credit bureaus' radar, you need to do two things. You need to show that you're responsible about paying your bills, and you need to have other people vouch for you.

Under normal life circumstances for a person established in the working world, you're showing this proof (or lack of it) yourself. You make payments on a mortgage or a car loan and thus show that you're able to manage your credit cards responsibly. By building up a track record over the years with different companies, you're essentially getting them to vouch for your future behavior.

But if you haven't had any of those accounts before, you really can't show a good payment record. And you need somebody else to vouch for you until you can vouch for yourself. If you want to take your credit from 0 to 700 in 90 days, that comes in the form of authorized users and secured credit.

Let's talk about authorized users first. Historically, it has been in the credit card companies' interest to find easy sources of new customers. They can (and do) spend a lot of money marketing their products with the hope that somebody will ditch a Capital One card for an American Express, or vice versa. That's why you see card company names all over college football bowl games, NFL team stadiums, and concert tickets around the country.

A cheaper way of getting customers to do this is to let current customers add authorized users to their accounts. This has a whole list of benefits for everybody involved. The credit card companies get a new card in a new customer's hand, which hopefully means some more spending. The customer (hopefully) has done some vetting of the person they're adding, so they're getting a responsible authorized user. The authorized user is getting the benefit of tagging along on another account in good standing, which helps their credit score — and leads them to eventually be able to get their own account. With many credit cards, an authorized user gets the benefit of the account holder's full history with the card — years and years of positive payment history and credit management, in ideal cases. That's a big, big deal.

The system was originally created as a way for stay-at-home wives and children to have access to the central credit card account, and it still works very well for this purpose. It also works great for a kid entering the working world who might need a hand with their credit.

The mechanical process to add an authorized user couldn't be easier. You simply call up your credit card company with the name, Social Security number, and address of the person you want to authorize to use your account.

The decision to do this — either as the person who asks or the person who gets asked — is more complicated. If you're asking somebody to add you as an authorized user, there obviously needs to be a level of trust there. You want to ask somebody who knows you and can trust that you won't abuse the favor. As the person asking, you also want to make sure of some technical considerations on the account you're asking to join.

The accounts that are going to benefit you the most have very specific characteristics:

- Open for at least two years
- A low utilization rate (less than 10 percent of the credit limit)
- No late payments in the last three years
- Be in good standing
- Report to all three credit bureaus (for a constantly updated list of creditors that report to all three, visit the book section of my website, anthonymdavenport.com/yourscore)
- Report a full credit history (some companies, like American Express, report only from the time the authorized user was added)

It's obviously a delicate conversation to have, but if everybody is up front about the process, it can go smoothly. If you're the person adding the authorized user, you don't have to physically give the user a card for use on the account. It's enough to simply add them for reporting purposes, and you don't have to worry about somebody going on an unauthorized shopping spree.

Getting added to two accounts as an authorized user within the first month of the "credit slam" will give you very positive credit within 60 days. For the purposes of the credit bureaus, it's as if you opened the accounts yourself.

The second prong of the slam process is to add two *secured* credit cards within that first 30-day window. Secured cards aren't a mystery. Various companies will let you send them cash, which will then be converted into the same amount of credit on a card — instead of extending you a conventional credit line like a regular credit card. There's no risk to the secured card issuer, because you're essentially spending the same money that you sent it. It charges you an annual fee for the privilege (and you're essentially spending your own money up front), but the cards are then reported to the bureaus as revolving debt — and if you pay back what you spend each month, you're building positive credit and establishing that you can handle money.

I tell my clients that these kinds of cards aren't for walking around. You're not whipping out your secured card to buy coffee at Starbucks or do online shopping at Amazon. You merely want to show small, regular purchases each month and then clear those purchases by redepositing your cash up to the secured limit religiously. Set the cards up to pay your Netflix or Spotify bill, and link them up to your checking account to automatically get zeroed out every month.

The best secured cards — Capital One has a good one that will let you deposit $200 to $3,000 up front, with no annual fee — have the ability to convert to an unsecured card once you show a pattern of on-time repayment. Then the training wheels can come off, so to speak.

After 90 days, you'll show four different trade lines reporting to the credit bureaus. You won't be getting much help from the secured cards yet, but they'll add the variety of accounts the bureaus are looking for. If you don't have any other dings on your credit report from late payments, you can expect that your score will be in the 700s at that point.

Once you get there, it's time to start applying for some of the prime unsecured cards, like an American Express Platinum or a Chase Sapphire Preferred card. If your score is in the 700–720 range or above, you should be approved. Once you've been approved and you get to the one-year mark, you can then request to be removed as an authorized user from your initial two accounts. It's a courtesy to the people who have been generous enough to help you out, and it also protects you. That way, if your friend or relative goes through their own financial problems, those issues will not be reflected in your scores.

The Slow and Steady Plan

Not everybody has access to the easy early boost that an authorized user account provides. If you don't have the network to help you out in that capacity, you can still put yourself in a good credit position in nine months to a year.

The advice about opening secured cards is the same as for the slam plan. Start out by getting two of those cards going right away, secured by as much cash as you can spare. You can also go to your bank or credit union and ask them for an installment loan backed by a certificate of deposit. That's just a fancy way of saying you'll give the bank a certain amount of money on deposit, and they'll loan you the same amount of money. There's no risk to the bank, and they collect some fees and interest. Meanwhile, in return, you get an installment loan reporting to the bureaus.

After nine months with the secured cards and installment loans, go to your secured credit card companies and ask them to convert your cards to being unsecured. If they decline, request that the limits be raised so you can fund the accounts with more cash — which is essentially raising your credit limit. When you make the request, they'll examine your payment history, your credit score, and your income to see how you're doing. If you stick with this plan and don't have more than five credit lines open, you're most likely going to get approved for the unsecured card.

The financial crisis of the late 2000s pushed many people into less-than-ideal financial circumstances, but it also created a large market for "unconventional" services geared toward the folks in those kinds of predicaments. For example, if you make regular cell phone or rent payments — which aren't normally included on credit reports from the bureaus — you can go through different programs administered by the federal government via the Community Reinvestment Act, which is designed to get people in disadvantaged communities approved for loans. The banks in that program can use your payment record on your cell phone or cable bill to help establish your creditworthiness. There are obviously restrictions on the plan, but you can contact your local bank to obtain more information and see if you qualify. There are also companies that essentially sell you a spot as an authorized user on a line of credit. That tends to be an expensive option, but it's one to consider if you're running into obstacles with some of the other strategies. Some of my clients have used SuperiorTradeLines.com and have had good results.

*

The endgame for either of these processes depends on what your goal is. If you're trying to get into position to qualify for a car loan, you should be able to secure one after six months of effort and a score in the 700s, provided you have the income to back up the car you're trying to buy. But mortgages are a different story, especially these days. Originators want to see credit lines at least two years old, which makes your authorized user accounts very important.

You can troll around the internet and find all kinds of vague tips about establishing credit, but I can tell you from firsthand experience with clients (and myself) that the relatively unsexy strategies I'm promulgating here actually work.

The basketball player we talked about at the beginning of the chapter? We went to the collection agency that had purchased his medical debt and inquired about the legitimacy of it. We wanted to make sure it was actually his and then formulate a strategy for dealing with it. The creditor volunteered a bunch of information about the doctor and treatment — which is a clear violation of medical confidentiality rules. We then made a deal with the creditor to forget about the confidentiality violation and to exchange the money that was owed for a complete deletion of the debt from the bureaus.

Once we had a clean slate, we followed the 90-day plan laid out in this chapter. By the end of the third month, the player had moved into a new condominium, signed up for car insurance on his $185,000 Bentley at a competitive rate (which is still nuts), and he was well on his way to being able to qualify for an American Express black card.

Life at the Other End . . .

Speaking of black cards, you might be wondering what it takes to get one. American Express keeps the criteria secret, but I've gotten some inside intelligence from friends on the other side of the business about the general parameters.

The first step is being one of American Express's top-tier Platinum cardholders. You should have a history with American Express of at least a year and a credit score of at least 760. Those qualifications are probably the easiest to hit.

The spending and income ones are a bit more exclusive. American Express's algorithms need to predict your annual spending on the card to be at least $250,000, preferably more than $350,000. You're going to need an income in the millions and a net worth in the multiple millions. The spending amounts increase for business accounts. Typically, a minimum of $350,000 must be spent on business accounts in order to be considered.

Get over those hurdles and the $7,500 initiation fee and the $2,500 annual fee shouldn't be a problem. If you want to be considered, call American Express's Centurion line at 800-956-9293 and ask for your interest to be noted. Someone there will monitor your account, and you can be sure that they'll Google your name, too — because the card has marketing requirements to go with the financial requirements. The card is a status symbol, and if you're playing a sport professionally or star in concerts on television, you have a much better chance of scoring one.

Trust me when I tell you that it's way harder on a client's ego to be turned down for not being famous enough than it is to miss on the financials.

Higher Education: Navigating the School Loan Landscape

THE WORD "BUBBLE" IS a popular concept these days in the media. It's often used to describe an economic situation where the underlying fundamentals cause a painful contraction in the market. In the early 2000s, we saw it in the stock market with dot-com companies that were on the bubble and then again in the housing market with the subprime loan crash. These days, if you're looking for the biggest bubble of the 2010s, student loans are probably the best place to start. Why?

Because the total student loan tab in the United States is more than $1.5 *trillion*. That's double the outstanding amount on every credit card in every American consumer's wallet or purse and $500 million more than the outstanding balance on every car loan currently issued.

That $1.5 trillion number is a scary figure, but what's even scarier is that students have racked up that debt in one of the most favorable borrowing environments in history — at least in terms of interest rates. If you borrowed money in the last ten years, you did it at historically low rates. It wasn't uncommon to lock in rates between 3 and 4 percent for federally subsidized undergraduate school loans in 2013 and 2014.

As anybody who locked in a mortgage during that time knows, rates have only gone up since then. And it is likely that we're going to see an extended period of interest rate increase over the next five to ten years. True, the interest rate you pay on your student loans is usually locked in from the time you signed up for the loan, but every new loan being written is coming at a higher rate — and the ability to refinance loans at historically low rates is probably gone for at least a decade.

That means that more students are going to come out of school with larger student loan bills than ever before, and with the rising costs of tuition and interest, they'll be paying more toward those loans than ever before. Students graduating with a bachelor's degree in 2016 came out with an average of more than $31,000 in student debt. If those payments aren't deferred, that means a person with an entry-level job is paying at least $320 a month on a school loan for ten years.

It doesn't take a degree in mathematics to see that not much has to go wrong for that person making $25,000 or $30,000 a year to really struggle to pay that college loan debt. And that debt load is a *huge* reason why borrowing among people ages twenty-five and under is at levels we haven't seen since the 1940s.

Look at it this way. If you're taking home $19,000 on a $25,000 salary after taxes, you have about $1,600 a month to pay for your life. After rent, cable, internet, and some money for beer and pizza, there isn't much left. And many, many people are getting hit with student loan reality years after they graduate, when they hit a bump in the employment road. All of a sudden, their income stream isn't what it was, and they begin to fall behind on the payments. With almost 50 million Americans holding some kind of school debt and that number growing by 10 percent every year, it's an issue that isn't going away.

College tuition is going up much faster than salaries are, and interest rates aren't going to help you out as much as they have.

Which means if you have student loans now, you need a good strategy to figure out how to handle the debt load — and restructure your payments if you need more breathing room.

Let's start with some student loan basics.

If you've been through the process, you already know the drill. The sticker price on an average year of college — tuition, room, and board — in 2016 was $20,000 for in-state public schools, $35,000 for public out-of-state schools, and $45,000 for private schools. Unless you're lucky enough to have parents who can write a big check, you're going to have to cover those costs with a combination of scholarships and student loans.

Student loans come in two broad forms: federal loans and private loans. Federal loans like Stafford, Perkins, and William D. Ford Direct Loans are administered by the U.S. government (either through funding directly from the government or by being guaranteed by the government and issued by a bank or school), and they don't rely on the student's (or parents') credit score, income, or grades. Private loans are offered by banks and credit unions, and they're subject to all the same rules and restrictions the lender would require for any other loan. In most cases, a younger student would need a parent to cosign for the loan because they wouldn't have established credit or income to cover the payments. Students going to school later in life will probably also need a cosigner in the form of a spouse or significant other if their income is going to be affected by going to school.

Federal loans come in two flavors — subsidized and unsubsidized. Subsidized loans are determined by a need-based formula, and the interest payments are covered by the government while the student is in school, as well as for a six-month window after graduation. You need to be an undergraduate student enrolled for at least half of a full course load to qualify for a subsidized loan. Unsubsidized loans are available to undergraduate *and* graduate students regardless of need, and they require the student to pay the interest on the loan starting immediately. Once the student graduates, they then begin to make principal payments.

To get a federal loan, you fill out a complicated set of financial paperwork through your soon-to-be-college that measures how much you and your family can be expected to contribute toward your undergraduate education. (You can also qualify for federal student loans for graduate school.) If you don't have much income or have a bunch of siblings in school at the same time, you're going to register more need than a student with more family income or fewer expenses.

At the end of that process, you'll find out how much in federal student loans you're eligible to take out. That number will depend on your year in school (and the dollar amount is changed by Congress periodically) and whether or not you can be claimed as a dependent by your parents. Those loans are chopped up into a variety of subsidized and unsubsidized programs. For example, if you are a freshman and have no family income to contribute and are supported by your parents, you might qualify for the full $9,500 in federal and federally backed loans, with a maximum of $3,500 in subsidized loans. By the time you are a senior, you can qualify for up to $12,500, of which $5,500 can be subsidized. The current caps on loans are a total of $31,000, of which $23,000 can be subsidized. If your parents don't qualify for a particular loan program that allows them to borrow for you, you can receive up to $57,500. We're going to talk about cosigners and co-borrowers later in this chapter.

The interest rates for the various federal and federally backed loans are also set by Congress. Right now, they range between about 4 and 6 percent, but as I said earlier, we're near historic lows in interest rates, and those numbers are probably going to go up in the near term. You can do math, so it's obvious that $18,000 doesn't cover all the costs of going to school. To make up the difference, you would need to come up with scholarship money, get a job, or go through a bank or credit union to take a private loan.

Private loans are different than federal ones in that they're backed by the banking institution and its investors, not the government. Federal loans have some significant advantages over private loans, but that comes with a very significant caveat. Federal loans almost always have lower interest rates than private loans, and the federal loan programs are much more flexible about renegotiating the terms of your loan down the road if you run into a hardship. But if you default on a federal loan, you're automatically disqualified for virtually any other federally backed loan program — which includes many mortgages for first-time homebuyers. You also can't escape federal school loans through bankruptcy. They're going to be with you until you pay them off. We're actually reaching the point where people are carrying school loan debt into retirement. The government had to make rules establishing that your Social Security benefits can be garnished by up to 15 percent of the monthly total if you go into default. The Government Accountability Office found that students who got to retirement with student loan debt carried a balance of approximately $10,000 on average and ended up having to pay about $140 out of their monthly benefits. Yes, you read that right. Some borrowers have refinanced and pushed their payments so far down the line that they still have a student loan balance when they get to retirement age.

Private loans can be defaulted upon and cleared through a bankruptcy, which means the lenders charge more in interest to price in that risk. Rates for private loans come in around 9 to 12 percent — 5 to 6 points higher than federal or federally backed loans. On a $10,000 loan with a ten-year term, that's the difference of about $25 a month.

Committing to a series of student loans is a lot like signing up for a mortgage. You have to do a fair bit of predicting the future —

which can be scary. For a mortgage, you have to figure out if you can afford the payments over the long term and if the amount of money you're borrowing is worth the house you're getting in return. School loans work the same way. You have to make an estimate about your earning potential when you graduate and decide if the weight of your student loans will be covered by that potential income stream. I'm not making any judgments about a degree in journalism or art history, but those fields offer lower starting salaries than fields like electrical engineering or human resources. The website Salary.com does a good job giving you rough estimates about starting salaries for various professions.

What many students end up with after four or five years of undergraduate work (or more, if you tack on a graduate degree) is a patchwork of loans serviced by a variety of different providers — loan servicing companies contracted by the U.S. Department of Education or the private bank or credit union you used to get your loan. One of the biggest initial stumbling blocks for students fresh out of school is — believe it or not — keeping an accurate tally of what they owe and who to pay. Add in the normal transition to a different address away from school and the distractions that come with jumping into the work world and it's easy to see how plenty of students get into a hole almost immediately.

The first step is to come up with a complete roster of the student loans you owe. You have a few different avenues to pull this information together. You can call the financial aid office at your school, and you can pull a copy of your credit report to see a list of your creditors. You can also work through the National Student Loan Data System — the official clearinghouse for all federal and federally backed loans. It's a good idea to go to all three sources and make sure the information matches up and go through the process of unifying the information if there are any mistakes. You can use the strategies in Chapter 4 to make sure the information on your credit report is accurate. The National Student Loan Data System gets its information from schools, which makes it really useful if you've accumulated loans while studying at more than one college or university.

When you first move into the real world and have to start paying on those loans, it can come as a shock. The dollar figures on the loans can seem almost like Monopoly money when you're signing for them, and because they come due in what seems like a long way into the future, they're much more abstract than real. But handling those loans correctly from the beginning is extremely important, because for most young people, those loans represent the vast majority of their credit history.

In other words, you come out of school with very little exposure to the world of consumer credit. If you're trying to get a job or even sign up for your own cell phone plan, you're going to get your credit pulled. If the only thing creditors (or potential employers) see is a bunch of missed and delinquent payments right from the get-go, you're going to have some problems.

The basic federal or federally backed student loan has a repayment term of ten years, with 120 identical payments. You do have a variety of repayment options (and refinancing and consolidation options, which we'll talk about later) to fit your situation. The most common modification is the "extended" plan, which keeps the same ten-year term but starts your initial payment at a lower figure and increases it through the life of the loan.

The other plans take into consideration your income and cap your payment as a percentage of your discretionary pay. The downside is that most extend the term of the loan up to nineteen and a half years from the standard ten. Plans like PAYE (Pay as You Earn), REPAYE (Revised Pay as You Earn), and IBR (Income-Based Repayment) call for a payment of 10 percent of your discretionary income. The ICR (Income-Contingent Repayment) plan is capped at 20 percent of your discretionary income or your payment amortized over twelve years on the standard repayment plan, whatever is less.

The Department of Education provides detailed information for each of these plans on its student aid website (studentaid.ed.gov) and offers a detailed look at how a new graduate with $25,000 in income and $30,000 in direct, unsubsidized loans can modify their payments. Under a standardized repayment plan (which starts immediately, as compared to a subsidized plan that starts payments after graduation), the student would owe $333 per month for ten years. Under a graduated repayment plan, the payments start at $190 and slowly escalate to $571 per month over that ten-year span. By moving into the PAYE, REPAYE, or IBR plans, a student can cut his or her initial payments to $60 a month. They eventually climb to $296 over the new twenty-year life of the loan. Under ICR, the payments change to $195 to start and gradually increase to $253 over the nineteen and a half years of the loan. The benefit of the PAYE and REPAYE plans is that they include some interest forgiveness — the government lops off a chunk of interest while you still pay the principal over a longer period of time.

To get into any of the repayment plans, you go to studentaid .ed.gov and fill out an application, which asks for a variety of financial information for you (and your spouse, if you're married). In general, your adjusted gross income from your latest tax return will be used, along with some other expense calculations, to determine your monthly disposable income. You'll have to document all of your income and expenses with things like W-2 forms, leases, and mortgage and car loan paperwork. It's important to note that your spouse's income and any expenses you'd incur because you have kids are considered in that calculation. Your spouse also has to cosign for the loan, which means they are also on the hook for it down the road if you can't pay.

Let's talk about exactly what happens if you *do* get into a jam with your student loans — either right after graduation or down the road a few years. Many, many student loan borrowers actually get more than halfway through their loan term in decent shape, but run into problems paying the loan when they encounter the setbacks that are a regular (and unfortunate) part of life — job loss, divorce, or a big medical bill hit. It's not a surprise why it happens. If you're choosing between a roof over your head, a major car repair, and paying toward your school loans, the school loan is going to be a lower priority.

And at least in the short term, that isn't a terrible strategy — at least if you're talking about federal or federally backed loans. Unlike, say, a mortgage or credit card account, or a student loan you've taken with a private lender — which will show up as a black mark on your credit if you go past 30 days delinquent — you won't be reported to the credit bureaus for delinquency on a school loan until you are at least 90 days past due. So if you're having a short-term cash-flow problem, you have more wiggle room with a school loan than a different account before you hurt your credit score.

But after 90 days, the delinquency starts to report to the credit bureaus, and when you get to 270 days delinquent — nine months behind on your payments — your account will be taken over by a collection agency. Even though your account is no longer being managed by a federal agency (or one of its designated loan servicers), the pain the collection agency can inflict on you is every bit as real — and much more severe than any credit card company or mortgage originator.

When your federal or federally backed student loan is delinquent, you are automatically kicked out of virtually any other loan program — which means you'll have an almost impossible time getting a mortgage or a car loan, and you will no longer be eligible for any of the government's deferment and forbearance plans. This is important, and we're going to talk more about it in a second. And the collection people with federal school loan debt go to the front of the line when it comes time to garnish your wages or your federal and state tax refunds — or even latch on to some of your Social Security benefits.

Because the consequences of defaulting on a federal or federally backed student loan are so severe — and because there are a variety of programs available to help you make it through a rough patch — it's crucial to address the problem early and head-on. When you get to the point of missing a payment because you just don't have the cash — as opposed to being careless or disorganized — reach out to the loan servicer *right away* and explain your situation.

Loan servicers working with federal loans are required to offer you several options for solving your delinquency, but those options disappear when the loan moves from delinquency to default. The first option is to rehabilitate your delinquent loan. You'll be asked to fill out an application and prove your income and expenses. If you're accepted into the rehabilitation program, you'll be required to pay nine monthly payments in a row on time (within 20 days of the due date) and pay an amount equal to 15 percent of your discretionary income. If you can make it through that nine-month probationary period, your loan comes back out of delinquent status and goes back to "normal," with the interest and principal you failed to pay over those nine months cooked back into the loan total. You'll be back in the good graces of the loan program and eligible for any of the deferment, forbearance, or consolidation programs we're going to talk about below. But there's a major caveat. You can only use the loan rehabilitation option once during the life of your loan. If you do use it, you need to get your finances in order and pick a long-term program that is going to work for your situation, because you won't get another bite of the apple.

One client decided to go back to school in her thirties. She was disillusioned with the corporate world, and she wanted to do something that would help people. Unfortunately, as she neared the end of her program, her husband told her he wanted a divorce. He was no longer going to contribute to paying those school loans, and they still had two kids to raise. When she graduated, she wasn't able to find a job right away, and when she did finally get work, it didn't pay enough to cover everything. She stopped paying on the loans for more than a year until she eventually came to me to help her do something about it. She converted to an income-based payment plan, and it gave her some room to get current on her debts. She still had to absorb the hit to her credit from all the late payments, but she managed to stop the bleeding. Within eighteen months, she had restored her credit to where it was before the divorce.

If you anticipate that you're going to go through a tough time — like a job loss or long-term treatment for an illness — or you're continuing your education at graduate school or going into the military, you can request a loan deferment or forbearance. A deferment essentially stops the clock on your loan for a period of time. If you get deployed overseas in the National Guard, for example, you can apply to have your student loans deferred until you come back. You can also get a deferment if you can't find a job. You can request deferments from your loan servicer, and the amount of time you can qualify to receive depends on your specific situation. For example, if you move on to graduate school, you can usually get a deferment for the length of time you're enrolled as a full-time graduate student. If you're unemployed, you can usually get a deferment for up to three years.

If you don't otherwise qualify for a deferment, you can request loan forbearance from your loan servicer. Forbearance is more in play when you have a job and income but you're just not able to cover your loans with the money you're making. With a forbearance, you can get up to twelve months to either skip payments or pay a reduced amount. But, like the deferment, the principal and interest you owe doesn't go away. The clock just starts up again when you come out of the period of forbearance.

A third option, loan consolidation, works a lot like a mortgage refinance on a house. You can work with your loan servicer to consolidate all of your student loans into one fixed-rate loan and extend the payments out for a longer period of time to lower your monthly payment. This has been an attractive option over the last five or six years because of historically low interest rates. The downside is the same as it would be if you extended your home loan over a longer period. You're going to pay much more in interest over the life of a thirty-year loan vs. a ten-year loan.

The process to consolidate federal or federally backed loans is simple. You apply for consolidation electronically at Student Loans.gov, and if you're current with all of your payments, you'll be given a single loan with an interest rate that is the weighted average of the interest rates of all the loans you're consolidating, plus 0.125 percent. You can keep the length of the loan the same as the loans you currently carry or extend them out to as long as thirty years. Be sure to examine the differences between the loans you currently carry and the one you would get through consolidation — especially given that we're going into a period of probable interest rate increases. If you have low fixed rates on many of your existing loans, it might not make sense to consolidate, even though it might be more convenient and mean less money out of pocket in the short term.

The World of Cosigners and Co-Borrowers

Federal loans essentially turn you into a grownup right away. You sign your name on them, and you're the one who will be responsible down the road. But if you need private loans to supplement those federal ones, you're going to need a cosigner. That usually means Mom or Dad, but it can also be a significant other. Helping a student make their education dreams come true is a generous thing, but I want to make sure you know what you're getting into if you're the one doing the cosigning.

As we've covered in the credit card and mortgage chapters, when you cosign student loan documents, you're what's known as jointly and individually liable for the debt. The debt servicer can and will come after both people named on the loan if it hasn't been paid. In the early days of the loan, the student probably doesn't have much money to come after, which means Mom or Dad (or husband or wife) are the ones who will be on the hook. But I've also seen plenty of cases in my practice when husbands and wives cosign for each other, only to break up later. Then, one of the ex-spouses stops paying on the school loan and leaves the other with a nasty surprise.

Late payments and defaults on cosigned student loans hit the cosigner's credit report exactly as they would for a car loan or any other type of debt. It doesn't matter if the student has dropped out of school, moved away, or stopped speaking to you! One very famous entertainer came to my office looking for a way to solve a cosigning situation that was wrecking her credit. She had agreed to help out a family friend, and the student graduated and stopped paying the loan. He didn't care about the damage to his own credit and didn't have any assets for anybody to go after. The only solution was to negotiate with the lender and pay off the bill — and try to recover the cash someday through a lawsuit.

Another client started a long-term relationship with a man who relocated from overseas to go to graduate school in New York City. He didn't have any money, and because he wasn't part of the American credit system, he couldn't qualify for any standard loans. They had been going together for a year, so my client decided she'd cosign for him on a private loan through her bank.

You can guess what happened. They broke up, and the man moved back to his home country, degree in hand. He stopped paying the loans and left my client holding the bill. Her ability to sue him — and collect — was limited by six thousand miles of distance and international borders. It was a hard $60,000 lesson for her to learn.

Relationships between parents and kids are obviously more permanent, but everybody needs to have a frank, open conversation about the loan and cosigning process before committing to a loan. Nobody wants to hear that their dream degree isn't a good investment, but given how much college costs, it is a reasonable conversation to have. If you're going to cosign for a loan for one of your children for tens of thousands of dollars, you do need to consider the potential marketability of that degree — and your child's ability to make enough money to cover those loan payments. Because if they can't, as the cosigner, you'll have to.

The career services office at your future college or university is a great place to visit before commencing an undergraduate or graduate degree. The vast majority of students wait until they're a year or two from graduating to take the temperature of the job market. You should be looking at school as an investment long before that — and researching what kind of return you could get on your degree *before* you make your loan commitments. When you're still in college is also a good time to be starting some other small forays into the credit world through the strategies we talked about in the last chapter — a small secured credit card or being added as an authorized user on a few accounts. You'll be getting a head start on building some accounts that will have some age on them.

I got a communications degree from Washington State University, and my cowriter earned his in journalism from Michigan State. At the time we went to school, the undergraduate tuition at both places was less than $9,000 per year. The average salaries in our degree fields were about $23,000 and $21,000, respectively. You can do some back-of-the-envelope math on your school loan numbers to see what kind of payment you could carry if you're bringing home $1,500 a month from your entry-level job. That math changes dramatically if you're getting a mechanical engineering degree from MIT or coming out of Harvard's MBA program.

The huge loan numbers that get thrown around can certainly be discouraging, but there is a silver lining to all of this school debt.

If you can come out of school and make responsible headway on paying your loans, you're establishing a strong foundation for your credit profile. As you come out of that standard ten-year debt term, a creditor looking at your profile and seeing almost a decade of regular, on-time payments sees somebody who is a responsible consumer and a good risk. It's not unusual for my clients to finish their school loans with a credit score in the high 700s — and all of a sudden, improved cash flow to qualify for a much nicer car or better mortgage.

Think of it as the light at the end of the tunnel.

11

....

Disaster Relief:
Surviving Divorce,
Foreclosure, and Bankruptcy

Please note: You should consult a lawyer and/or other finance professional for advice specific to your particular circumstances.

I SINCERELY HOPE YOU NEVER have to use the advice in this chapter, but the unfortunate reality is that pretty much everybody goes through some sort of adversity in their financial life.

From the start of the economic meltdown in 2007 to 2012, when we finally shook clear of it, more than four million American families went through a foreclosure. And it wasn't limited to just those folks who had "subprime" mortgages — the high-risk, high-interest-rate loans that were at the heart of the crisis. The truth is, more than twice as many regular homeowners lost homes in the collapse than people with subprime loans. The hard truth is that if the company you work for goes under and you lose your job, it doesn't matter what your interest rate is.

The bankruptcy picture was even worse. More than five million people filed for bankruptcy protection during that time. Bankruptcy happens to most people because of crushing medical debts. But during the crisis, it happened to plenty of Americans just because the rug got pulled out from an otherwise healthy and normal financial life.

As we talked about at the beginning of this book, I was one of those people. During the Great Recession, the mortgage origination business cratered, and I went from a normal guy who had a nice house, paid his bills on time, and had money in the bank, to being one of the people in those bankruptcy statistics.

There isn't much positive to say about those years, but one good thing to come out of them is that the stigma surrounding many of the financial crises that hurt people every day is starting to fade. When more than fifty million people go through a foreclosure, bankruptcy, short sale, or job loss, there are a lot of people in the same boat.

It's a big enough group that the various credit card companies, banks, and other creditors can't just throw those people away. There *is* financial life after a foreclosure, bankruptcy, or a divorce. You just have to understand the steps to recovery — and hopefully have a plan in place ahead of time.

This chapter is going to serve two purposes. Ideally, it's something you read before you ever find yourself in one of these situations. You'll be better prepared if something awful should happen, and the experience will be far less traumatic.

But I'm also very aware that plenty of people reach out for help only when they're already waist-deep in trouble. If you're in the middle of the storm and looking for a lifeline, I'm here to help, too.

I usually separate credit problems into two categories. There are "issues," like late payments, collections, high balances, and other dings on your credit scores. And then there are "crises." A crisis is something that threatens the very foundation of your financial life. You can limp along in life with a credit score in the 600s. But if you're going to lose your house, your financial portfolio, or your marriage, those are serious problems that require a different level of attention and action.

Here, we're going to address the four major crises that plague tens of millions of regular people every year: divorce, foreclosure, the rental trap, and bankruptcy.

Between 40 and 50 percent of marriages end in divorce, and it's the most common financial pothole people face. Even under the most amicable terms, if you and your spouse shared any part of your financial life, you're going to have to do some triage to protect and establish yourself as an independent entity.

When it comes to your home, if you fall behind on your mortgage payments to the point where you're going to lose your house to foreclosure, you're in an extremely stressful situation. There are also short-term problems to solve — like where you're going to live next — in addition to the ones that come when your credit gets crushed afterward.

Foreclosure is the big, sexy topic on all the blogs, but another crisis I see even more often in my practice is what I call the "rental trap." Many young people get out of college and move into the workplace without much of a credit history. Most landlords do credit checks as a basic part of doing business, and if you don't have a credit score, you're going to find it almost impossible to sign a lease. If you can get one, you're going to pay an extreme penalty in the form of high rent and big deposits. It doesn't have to be that way.

The last crisis is the granddaddy of them all. Bankruptcy happens when you get to the point where you don't think you have any hope of digging yourself out of your financial hole. Yes, it puts a ten-year scar on your credit score. But it doesn't have to be a death sentence. There are steps you can take on the first day after your bankruptcy case is discharged to start to get back on your feet, and you can be back in the consumer credit game in less time than it takes to elect a new president.

Dealing with a Divorce

Any of these crises are going to take you through the wringer emotionally, but divorce comes with its own rough edges. If you're married and dealing with a foreclosure or a bankruptcy, you have the closest person in your life working with you on your team. But in a divorce, it's the team itself that's breaking up.

Divorces obviously have plenty of issues to be sorted, from children to ownership of property. Financial issues are a big, big piece, and your mission is to avoid letting the difficult emotions of the situation push you into making careless mistakes. It's also very common to feel overwhelmed and sad and to avoid making decisions altogether. That's understandable, but if you're not careful, this kind of approach can also multiply into much larger problems down the road.

Some divorces come as a complete surprise, but if you and your spouse have talked about it and are headed in that direction, you're going to want to take some steps before the paperwork is actually filed. For example, if you don't have your own personal credit card account that isn't jointly held with your spouse, now is the time to apply for one. Take advantage of the current household income you have together — even if you aren't working — to present a more attractive case to the credit card company.

When the divorce is actually filed, you won't be able to legally hide assets from your spouse, but that doesn't mean you shouldn't have a separate bank account. You want to be the only one who has access to it, and it makes sense to move it to a totally different bank than the one where you might have had joint accounts.

This is also the right time to collect your credit reports from all three bureaus and give them a full examination. In the previous chapters, we've been talking about how to hunt down suspicious-looking entries, so you should be pretty well-trained on how to review this paperwork. This time, you're looking for accounts on which you and your spouse are jointly named. That's going to appear two different ways on various accounts. You're either going to be jointly responsible for a given account — say, a mortgage loan — or you'll be either the primary account holder or the authorized user on a credit account.

If you and your spouse hold a credit card account jointly, there's no way to separate the responsibility for that card. You'll have to cancel it, and that's something good to do as soon as you've formulated your own plan and set up your own individual accounts. The only exception to that rule is if one of you uses the card for basic living expenses. Be sure to discuss all of this with your divorce lawyer before cancelling that card.

For mortgage accounts and car loans, you'll have to do paperwork within the process of your divorce agreement to establish one person or the other as the owner of the actual asset (and the debt that goes with it) or determine that the asset needs to be sold and the proceeds (or remaining debt) allocated in some way.

On the other hand, with credit cards where you're the primary account holder and you have your spouse as an authorized user, it's as simple as calling the credit card company and having the authorized user removed. If you're the person who has been added as an authorized user, you're also going to want to call the credit card company and request to be removed.

It's not because of the potential for being liable for a bill, because you won't be. It's because your credit score is tied to that account. And if your soon-to-be-former spouse goes off the rails financially, they could take you down, too.

And really, that's the main thrust of all the advice in this book when it comes to dealing with a divorce. You might have the friendliest divorce of all time, but the reality is that you're no longer going to be tied to this person. As such, you don't want to leave yourself in a position where you could have your credit damaged by somebody who isn't living in the same house and isn't working as a member of your two-person relationship team. It doesn't mean you think they're dishonest or that they're trying to cheat you (of course, those kinds of things happen, too). Also, don't feel guilty about asserting yourself and protecting yourself. The goal is to separate your financial lives as cleanly as possible and to leave yourself open only to credit risks that you see and accept for yourself.

Regardless of how friendly your divorce is, go back to Chapter 8 and follow the steps for putting a security freeze on your files with all three credit bureaus. I wish I could say it wasn't all that common that burned, soon-to-be-former spouses opened new lines of credit and maxed-out credit cards out of anger. But it happens all the time, and you're especially vulnerable when somebody knows all of your pertinent information — passwords, security questions, mother's maiden name, high school mascot, etc.

One of the most common mistakes I see with my clients is that they think, for some reason, that the divorce decree will do all of this work for them. When things get settled in court, the divorce paperwork might say that your spouse is responsible for the debt incurred on the Amex you jointly hold. But the divorce decree doesn't void your agreement with the credit card company. If you don't personally close that account, Amex doesn't care that you're divorced. Your name is on the account, and even though the decree says your spouse is responsible for the debt, if they then run up another $10,000 and flake out on it, it will still show up on *your* credit report.

I can't stress it enough. Even if things are amicable and you have a good relationship with your soon-to-be-ex, you can be hurt very badly if you don't protect yourself by removing your name from accounts you don't control anymore. One client went through one of the friendliest divorces I've ever seen, from an extremely nice and responsible guy. During the process of the divorce — in which they didn't even use lawyers — they refinanced their home so that her name would come off the mortgage documents and sorted out all of the other assets between themselves. They didn't have kids, so they figured that was the end of it.

The problem? They had a joint credit card from Wells Fargo that he was responsible for paying. He never cancelled it, and years later, when he went through some lean times in his business, he fell behind on it. It was maxed out, and he missed several payments in a row. It went into collections, and Wells Fargo eventually closed the account.

My client didn't find out about this situation until she got a letter from one of her other credit card companies saying that her credit limit was being reduced. She came to me to find out why, and we checked her credit, which revealed this situation. Since the Wells Fargo account was closed, it was too late for her to remove herself from it. She had to live with the black mark, and it took years of work to recover.

Surviving a Foreclosure

This isn't the place to go into an in-depth discussion about *why* foreclosures happen. If you're reading this, you are either in the middle of it happening to you or worried that it might happen. The most basic reasons are usually job-related. Somebody loses a job and can't afford the house payments anymore, and they can't sell the home for close to what they owe on it. Other reasons are more insidious. If you had an adjustable-rate mortgage and you didn't fully understand what you were getting into, you could have been taken by surprise when the rate reset and jumped significantly after a certain number of years. All of a sudden, what used to be a comfortable payment became a major stretch.

Once you start missing payments, it doesn't take much to tip over the whole cart. Most people prioritize the roof over their heads before other bills, so they start by paying the mortgage at the expense of other bills, like credit cards. Then those start to become late and delinquent, and they never catch up. Once you miss a string of house payments and the penalties and late fees begin to add up, the mountain starts to look impossible to climb — especially if you happen to live in a market where real estate values are flat or have gone down.

One of the oldest clichés in real estate is that you don't make money when you sell. You make money when you buy. In other words, you make a smart investment in a house that cost you less than it's truly worth. You're insulated because you basically have bought built-in home equity.

It's a cliché because it's true — and it's true for a variety of reasons. Yes, buying a house you can afford and that presents good value is always terrific. But you also win on the buy by being very aware of the process of securing your mortgage.

Affordability is just one piece of the game, as we discussed in Chapter 6. Many, many people find themselves in foreclosure because they didn't sweat the small details during the mortgage process, and the mortgage originator wasn't in a hurry to help them out.

Need an example? When you go to an originator to get your mortgage, they are going to pull your credit. The credit report they pull becomes locked in for up to 90 days. Which means you better have done whatever repair work was needed on your credit *before* that first interaction with the originator. Once you're locked in and can't fix something — even something simple that could give you that 10-point boost on your credit score from the second tier to the first tier — you're going to be stuck with the interest rate that's spit out by the algorithm.

When you're working in a good job and have money in the bank, an extra $300 or $400 a month in interest on your mortgage payment doesn't seem like a big deal. But when you're just scraping by, it can mean the difference between keeping your house and losing it.

When you sign for a mortgage, you're basically exchanging your commitment to make payments over a certain period of time for the money to buy a house. If you don't keep up with your payments, the bank that holds your mortgage is going to come after you for either the money or your house. If it doesn't get your money, then it's going to take your house in foreclosure to sell off and make good on your debt.

It's obviously a scary and stressful situation. But having some information about how this all happens can help some of that stress go away. For example, if you're late on a mortgage payment, or even miss one or two payments, the bank isn't going to come and take your house. But, that being said, once you are three to six months behind, you're going to see most banks begin the foreclosure process.

The rules about foreclosure vary from state to state, but generally speaking, the bank has to go through several steps to show it tried to collect from you and that you failed to pay — a process that usually takes between ten months and two years. (It's important to check with a foreclosure defense attorney in your state, because you can buy yourself *years* of time, especially in a state that requires a judge to sign off on every foreclosure.) But once the process has been completed, your house is either sold at an auction or repossessed by the bank and sold by a Realtor in a traditional sale.

Throughout virtually all of the process, you can lift yourself out of it if you can find a way to become current with your payments. The bank doesn't want to foreclose, because it's a headache to do so, and the bank isn't in the business of owning and selling homes. The truth is it would much prefer that you simply paid up so that it didn't have to go through all of this.

But if and when you get to the point where you can't make your mortgage payments, your first step should be to contact the bank or company that holds your mortgage — which could well be a different place than where you originally got your mortgage — and let it know. You might be able to negotiate a modification to your loan that reduces the interest rate, extends the term, or removes penalties and fees to give you more time and a lower payment to cover the principal you owe.

You'll have to give the lender some details about your situation — your monthly income, your expenses, and your assets — and it'll determine if you qualify for a modification. The earlier you go through this process, the better your chances are for getting approved. If you've already missed a half dozen payments, the lender is probably going to be skeptical about ever being made whole. The sweet spot for this kind of negotiation is after you've missed the first payment and are 30 days behind. You are clearly having trouble, but you haven't gone into critical condition, so to speak.

If you don't get a modification (or a temporary forbearance, which gives you a certain number of months to make little or no payments in order to get back on your feet), you then have to prepare for the next step.

Your instinct might be telling you to simply stop paying your mortgage if you know you're going to go into foreclosure, but that's really not a great strategy in most cases. In the foreclosure process, the entire amount of your outstanding loan goes onto the ledger as your debt, in addition to a variety of fees and penalties. However your home is eventually sold, the amount it brings (minus more fees and penalties) is subtracted from that debt on your ledger. Depending on where you live (and the terms of your mortgage), that remainder doesn't just vanish. If you live in what's called a "recourse" state or you have recourse language in your loan agreement, you continue to owe the remainder, and the bank will chase you down for it.

Which means that continuing to pay at least *something* reduces that exposure — and shows good faith for the negotiations that come next. As the foreclosure process continues, you can get permission from your lender to put your house up for sale as a "pre-foreclosure." If the house sells for less than you owe on your loan, you can ask your lender to approve what's called a "short sale."

If the short sale is approved, that's a minor victory. It doesn't leave as much of a black mark on your credit as a foreclosure, but it's still pretty close. It is reported as a charge-off or debt settlement, which raises a big red flag for other creditors. And it stays on your credit report for seven years.

Depending on how short the sale was in comparison to what you owe the lender, the lender can either forgive the remainder of the debt or chase you for the deficiency. It's important to ask for real clarification in writing as to what happens to the leftover debt, because if it sticks around after the foreclosure, it works like any of your other debts. If you can't pay that deficiency, you're going to get another black mark on your credit — and probably get sued.

If you have a second mortgage on your home, this is the time to be extra cautious. Generally speaking, the holder of the second mortgage has to get in line behind the first mortgage holder in a foreclosure or a short sale, and there usually isn't enough cash left over after the closing to pay off that second mortgage. I've had many clients come to me years after a foreclosure because a giant collection showed up on their credit report — an action from the second mortgage holder from the foreclosure, who is looking to get paid back.

When you're negotiating the foreclosure or short sale, be sure to talk to that second mortgage holder and get it on board with what's happening, because if you don't, you're going to have to contend with it down the road. Some states have non-recourse laws, which actually prevent those lenders from chasing you for the leftover debt. You can check if your state is one of them with a simple Google search, "recourse laws by state."

If you can't sell the house and the foreclosure is going to go through, your goal is to preserve as much of your credit health as you can so you can start to rebuild. First of all, don't cancel any credit cards, because it will be much more difficult to get new ones after the foreclosure. Your credit card companies could well reduce your credit line, increase your interest rate, or flat out close your account, but you should be able to preserve at least some of the cards through the foreclosure.

Your next goal is to secure housing that fits into your new financial world. We're going to talk more in the next section about getting a rental with compromised credit, and that's an important piece as you move forward with your life.

You can expect your credit score to go down at least 150 points after the foreclosure, probably more if you went into it with a score above 740. That will put you deep in subprime territory for the beginning of your ten-year stretch, but if you follow the right steps, you can actually be "normal" within two years of the foreclosure.

Stay current on your bills, and in the first six months after the foreclosure, set as your goal adding two more lines of credit and making one of those a secured credit card. Online banks like Capital One and Discover will be happy to have your business — and charge you for it — because they've seen just how many people are in the same boat. It's a huge market. Just make sure those credit card companies report to all three credit bureaus, because many don't.

Your next step is to ask a relative or a good friend to add you as an authorized user on one of their credit cards in good standing. Obviously this needs to be somebody who can trust you and would be willing to give you a hand up.

The best account to be associated with is one with a long, positive credit history. Anything less than two years old doesn't have much impact on your credit score. For example, getting added by your parents to one of their mature credit accounts can instantly give you a credit history longer than you've been alive. They're essentially vouching for you to allow you back in from the cold.

You're obviously asking for a big favor from the card owner.

One way to give them some confidence about helping you out is to tell them you don't even need a copy of the card. That is, you will get the benefit of the credit history even if you never physically touch the card or use it. If they're considering this for you, give them your Social Security number, address, and date of birth to make the process easier and reassure them that there's no need to be secretive about it. The card companies are very familiar with this strategy, and there's nothing wrong with it.

Staying out of the Rental Trap

Recently, I had a meeting with a client who is a very prominent music industry producer with a No. 1 hit record to his name, just in the last couple of years. He's a young guy, and he decided he was going to go out and get his own place for the first time — instead of crashing with a bunch of roommates. He didn't have much in the way of a credit profile, but he had more than $1 million in the bank, so he figured he'd be good when it came to looking at some nice rental condominiums on the water.

But when he filled out the credit application for the rental, he received a bad surprise. The landlord rejected him immediately. It turns out that my client and his dad share the same name, but are junior and senior. Senior went through a rough patch and had been evicted from some apartments.

Those evictions (along with tax liens and other specialized penalties) show up on the real estate version of the credit report I described in Chapter 6. Because my client was accidentally mistaken for his dad in the reports, nobody would touch him as a renter. It sounds like a funny problem, but it wasn't so much for my client. He actually spent six weeks living day-to-day in Airbnb apartments while we tried to sort out this credit mess.

Actually, his case is not so different from ones I see every day in my practice. People who don't have much of a credit history

— either because they're young and new to the workforce or because they come from a different country, which isn't accounted for in the bureaus' algorithms — often have an extremely hard time finding a place to rent.

Sure, you can find some places where a landlord's only requirement for a new resident is to check the person up and down with an eye test. But those places don't tend to be the nicest, and they're way harder to find than conventional rental apartments or houses.

In most cases, you're going to fill out a credit application when you try to rent an apartment or a house. And if you fall short in your credit profile, you're going to have a difficult time.

Luckily, this crisis isn't a particularly hard one to cure. Anybody can immediately inherit some good credit by asking to be included as an authorized user on a friend or relative's credit card, as I described earlier. You can also go in and clean up your credit report by disputing any of the identity errors that show up. That's what we did with my client who was confused with his dad's credit history. After showing proof of identity, we disputed the report with the bureaus, and the issue was cleared up in about a month.

The first step bears repeating. Check your credit reports thoroughly before you go filling out rental applications. Make sure there are no mistakes on there — and make sure you actually have a credit score in the first place. That's the big problem many of the professional athletes I see in my office have. They're twenty-year-olds who have never had a real job, and all of a sudden they have $5 million in the bank but no credit score. If you have *no* score, go back to Chapter 9 and follow the steps to get into the game. With some work and some help, you can be in the 700s within 90 days. That's a long time to be sleeping on somebody's couch, but it beats the alternative!

If you're starting from a decent credit position, use an online budget estimating tool like the one at Mint.com to plug in your income and expenses and get a ballpark affordability figure. Knowing how much you can spend on rent (or a mortgage payment) is a great reality check, because staying between the lines there is going to take pressure off all the other payments you need to make in a given month.

When you know what payment neighborhood you can be in, that's a good time to check in with a real estate agent who specializes in rentals. They can obviously help you find a good spot, but just as importantly, they're a great source for intel on the credit and income requirements of different buildings and condo complexes. Knowing where you have a chance to qualify makes the search way more efficient.

For example, I live in New York City, so I know that renting a place in a doorman building on the Upper East Side is going to take a huge income — on the order of forty times the annual rent payment — and a credit score in the 700s. If you have some issues in your credit history, a small-scale, private landlord with a single apartment to rent is going to be more open to hearing your explanation than a management company.

What's the bottom line in terms of the difference in dollars? Doing the dirty work to rebuild your score can keep you from having to pay twelve months of rent in advance — plus a security deposit. You'll be thrilled to get back to the world where you only need first month, last month, and one month of security deposit.

Digging out of a Bankruptcy

When I see new clients in the toughest of financial situations — with lots of creditors and stacks of delinquencies and late payments, or in the aftermath of a catastrophic business failure — they usually come around to asking me the same question during our first meeting.

"Should I declare bankruptcy?"

I'm not going to sugarcoat anything. A bankruptcy is a devastating event for your credit. It's an announcement to your creditors that you've given up, and you won't be paying them back, and it will make future creditors very, very cautious about dealing with you.

Depending on what kind of bankruptcy you declare — Chapter 7 and Chapter 11 are the two most common — you'll either have all or most of your unsecured debt wiped away at the end of the process. The good news is that you won't be paying toward your credit cards anymore, and you'll avoid having to pay any legal judgments against you from a creditor. In most cases, you'll also be able to keep your house — although if you can't afford those payments, you're going to eventually have to either sell the house or go through a foreclosure.

It's important to note what *doesn't* get discharged in a bankruptcy. For example, school loans backed by the federal government stick around, as do any tax liens you owe to your town, state, or the IRS.

Whether or not you should go through the bankruptcy process depends on the viability of your "way out." A lot of cases are no-brainers. I saw a client last week who had lost his job as an executive at a media company, and he was facing medical collections of more than $60,000. He was delinquent on all of his credit cards and was looking at another $85,000 in debt there. He had found another job, but it paid half of what he was making before. With three kids and all the expenses that come with them, there was just no way he was ever going to be able to get out of that hole without filing for bankruptcy. He really had no choice.

However, it's the borderline cases where you need to do some serious evaluation. The temptation is certainly there to pull the trigger and wipe away those debts — especially if you've already damaged your credit badly by going deeply into the hole in the first place. But if you go completely delinquent on a credit card with a big balance and it is sent to collections, you can clean that black mark much more easily than you can by resorting to a bankruptcy.

Bankruptcy is a big stick, and you should only choose it if there really is no viable path to resolving your debts in any other way.

There is no one-size-fits-all benchmark you should look at when trying to make the decision, but I like to start by examining the relationship between unsecured debt and your income. In my experience, if you have more unsecured debt than you do take-home income — and you could pay your mortgage if the unsecured debt were to be cleared — you're a good candidate for bankruptcy. The bankruptcy, while painful, gives you a chance to quickly rebuild a sustainable life.

Another very important factor in your decision is your particular state's bankruptcy exemption rules. When you file in your state, a certain amount of your property and equity in a home and vehicle are shielded from the bankruptcy. The amount of equity you have and where you live are going to play a big part in whether or not you should file. For example, Connecticut lets you protect up to $75,000 in equity in your home and $13,500 in equity in your car. But in Florida, you can protect unlimited home equity and $1,000 in car equity. Do some research, and consider talking to a bankruptcy attorney to get an accurate sense of your state's laws.

If you do decide to go through the bankruptcy process, let's talk about the functional changes that are going to happen to your financial life and what steps you need to start taking. In most cases, you fill out an affidavit that lists all the accounts you're including in the bankruptcy filing. Those would include all of your unsecured creditors, like credit card companies. Once you file, those accounts will instantly be closed by the creditors. But even if you have a clean record (so to speak) with one credit card company and don't include it in the bankruptcy proceeding, that creditor will almost always cancel your account immediately as well, because you've just shown that you aren't going to pay your bills.

Practically speaking, this means you're going to have to function in the short term without any credit. That means you're going to have to run an all-cash personal economy, which isn't so easy to do these days. You'll have a hard time renting a car, booking a hotel room, or doing a bunch of the other small things we take for granted these days when we use plastic.

A big part of dealing with the bankruptcy is the stigma that comes with it. If you're looking for a rental home or apartment, you're going to have to submit to a credit check when you fill out an application. A bankruptcy doesn't look great. Your best bet is to write a letter explaining your situation and outline your job situation and any other factors that would be reassuring to a landlord — or just move into a new place before the actual bankruptcy is filed.

Also bear in mind that anybody you list as a creditor — whether that's American Express or your uncle Jim — is going to be notified that you've filed. And bankruptcy records are public, which means that anyone interested in looking them up will see exactly what happened to you.

Your job universe can also be negatively affected by filing for bankruptcy. Many companies do a credit check as part of a hiring routine, and you're going to be judged by what's on your report. Some jobs specifically exclude people who have had financial problems like a bankruptcy. You won't be able to get a license to be a mortgage banker, for example, if you have a bankruptcy on your record.

You should also prepare yourself for the deluge of mail and email you're going to get from furniture stores, payday loan companies, and other bottom-feeders looking to profit on your tough times. The credit bureaus actually sell lists of struggling consumers to companies looking to market to that group. (You can check my website, www.anthonymdavenport.com/yourscore, for the links that will let you opt out of all the direct mail and phone marketing nonsense.)

The official "penalty" from a bankruptcy lasts ten years on your credit report. Which means that for ten years, creditors will be able to see that you've filed for bankruptcy protection. But the hit you take on your actual credit score records most heavily early on, right after the bankruptcy takes place. Just like any other black mark on your credit, that hit will recede over time — especially if you do things to improve your underlying score.

You will probably not be able to qualify for any kind of mortgage for four years after a bankruptcy, foreclosure, or short sale, so I tell my clients to look at that time period as the true "penalty box." You have four years to get things in order so that, when the time comes, you have some options for what to do next.

On day one after the bankruptcy, you can do the things we discussed in the last section about recovering from a foreclosure. Get yourself a secured credit card, and try to be added as an authorized user on a friend's account. One caveat to that strategy is that you won't be able to do business with American Express — even as an authorized user — if they were one of the creditors that got discharged in your bankruptcy. Unfortunately, the Amex guys have a long memory.

When you get your secured credit card, use it every month for a series of small transactions, and make sure to make the full payments owed every month. After a year, you can go to the issuer and ask for the card to be converted into an unsecured card. Start small — a $500 line isn't much risk for the creditor, and it is probably going to be willing to convert it for you if you've shown good payment habits for a year. You don't even have to take the card out of the envelope. Set it to pay something small, like your monthly Netflix bill, and zero it out every month with an automatic draw from your checking account. You'll show regular activity with a low utilization rate — exactly what the credit bureaus like to see.

A year out of bankruptcy, you should be able to qualify for a car loan from a "lower tier" automaker but with a significantly higher-than-average interest rate. By lower tier, I mean a car company that is aggressively doing deals to try to attract customers. You're not going to be able to walk into the local Lexus or BMW dealership and get a five-year loan at 3 percent, but the Mitsubishi or Volkswagen shop will probably be willing to give you a chance at 10 percent. A car loan is a good start because it's a collateralized loan. If you don't pay, the creditor gets back an asset that it can sell.

Some new online services are starting to pop up that cater to folks in this exact situation. If you've been through a bankruptcy, but you've since been paying your rent on time every month, you can go through a site like RentReporters.com and request that that payment history be entered onto your credit report. It isn't reported to all three credit bureaus, but it will be seen as a small victory by having it reported to one of the bureaus.

Through all of this, you might have noticed that I haven't mentioned anything about consumer credit counseling or debt consolidation services. I'm sure you've heard the radio ads for what they offer. Basically, you pay them a set monthly fee, and they go to work on your creditors to get them to settle for less than you owe.

The reason I haven't suggested them is because they're almost universally terrible for your credit situation. Bankruptcy is never something to take lightly, but in many cases you're honestly better off filing for that than working with a debt consolidation service or credit counselor. At least in the bankruptcy, the pain has an end date.

This is how it goes down when you sign up for one of those services. They go through your credit report, look at the creditors you owe, and come up with a fee to collect for their services. They'll take your money and pool it into an account, then call up each of your creditors, one by one. They'll tell the first one they won't be getting paid, and your late payments, fees, and penalties will continue to accumulate. They'll do the same thing with the second creditor, until they get to one with which they feel like they can negotiate. For that one, they'll offer pennies on the dollar to settle for less than you owe. Then they'll go back to the others — which have been marking you as delinquent for months now — and give them take-it-or-leave-it offers.

At the end of the day, you might have gotten out of paying a few thousand dollars toward your debts, but you've now dropped a bomb on your credit. Your creditors have all marked you down as somebody who dodged payments through a debt consolidator, and all of those late payments and charge-offs are still on your credit.

In bankruptcy, you take the poison and become radioactive for a certain amount of time, but then . . . it's over. With credit counseling or debt consolidation, you've taken the same poison, but you're still left with all the underlying problems for a long, long time. It's a bad, bad move.

Like I said, there's no way to sugarcoat a bankruptcy. This will be an embarrassing and frustrating time for you, but you can't let those emotions push you into a hole. It's like dealing with a giant hole in the roof of your house. You can decide that you don't want to deal with that hole, but next week, the hole is still going to be there. Plus, all of your furniture, carpeting, and possessions are going to be wet.

The sooner you accept your predicament and take the steps to get out of it, the closer you'll be to exiting the other side with decent credit. I've been through it myself. Within two years, I had unsecured credit cards and a car loan. Three years after, my credit was back to average. There's no reason why you can't do the same with these steps.

But if you wallow in the emotions, remain in denial, and hesitate in taking the steps we've been talking about, you'll look up in five years to find that you're still at the bottom. Credit is such an integral part of modern life that you can't afford to be out of the game for that long — not with basic non-financial transactions like job interviews and insurance quotes relying on your score as much as the financial stuff does.

You can do it.

Acknowledgments

FIRST AND FOREMOST, I WANT to thank my wife, Crystal Davenport, for always believing in our mission to help people better manage their credit. Not many spouses would support a new business endeavor immediately after we had lost everything and had a new baby to support. It would have been impossible to wholly dedicate myself to learning everything I possibly could about credit without her sacrifice. Countless hours were spent (many of them on evenings and weekends) attempting to pull back the curtain on the hidden credit world. Thank you most importantly for our three beautiful little boys, Jackson, William, and Carter, whom all this hard work is for. Thank you to Margaret and Craig, who raised a wonderful woman.

My generation is standing on the shoulders of giants, and I am no exception. My parents, Lawrence and Cecelia, instilled the nonstop work ethic and focus that drive me today. Their generation's ability to break down barriers in the face of overwhelming adversity left mine with no excuse but to seek greatness no matter how hard the climb. Thank you for believing in me long before anyone else did; I am honored to have you as my parents.

Special thanks to David Epstein, who inspired me to want to share all I have learned with the world and introduced me to my agent, Farley Chase, who connected me with Matt Rudy. We made a great team and I'm immensely grateful and proud of what we have accomplished. Too many people helped along the way; some but not all: Christina Morales (my right hand for seven awesome years), Evan Jehle, Mark Maimon, Sarah Valdovinos, and D. O.

Appendix

YSCS

YOUR SCORE
CREDIT SERVICES, INC.

123 Main Street
Anywhere, USA 12345
www.yscs.com

Tel: (555) 123-4567
Fax: (555) 123-5678
Email: info@yscs.com

PREPARED FOR
Dewey, Cheatem & Howe Bank
ONE NOWHERE PLAZA, ANYWHERE USA

Attention:	SMITH	**Prepared By:**		**Report Type:**	CHECKBOX INFILE
Reference #:	ABCSM-3000238	**Request Date:**	6/26/2018	**Sources:**	TU, EFX and XPN
Password:	Mb3pzynC7j	**Completed Date:**	6/26/2018	**Loan Type:**	
Client Loan #:	DOE, JOHN	**Client #:**	619	**ECOA Type:**	INDIVIDUAL
				Price: $ 7.65 Tax: $ 0.00 Total: $ 7.65	
AUS Reference #:					
Loan Officer:	IM GREATEST				

Applicant Information

Applicant:	DOE, JOHN	DOB:	01/01/1980
		SSN#:	012-34-5678
Street Address:	1060 WEST ADDISON ST.	Marital Status:	
City, State, Zip:	CHICAGO, IL 60613	Own/Rent:	
Length of Time:		Dependants:	
Property:			

Pulse	Check-Up

Score Information

EFX BEACON 5.0   **565**   Range 300 to 850   FOR: DOE, JOHN
Score Date: 06/26/2018   EFX-1

38   SERIOUS DELINQUENCY, AND DEROGATORY PUBLIC RECORD OR COLLECTION FIELD
18   NUMBER OF ACCOUNTS WITH DELINQUENCY
13   TIME SINCE DELINQUENCY IS TOO RECENT OR UNKNOWN
14   LENGTH OF TIME ACCOUNTS HAVE BEEN ESTABLISHED

TU FICO CLASSIC 04   **565**   Range 336 to 843   FOR: MORGAN, CHRISTIAN
Score Date: 06/26/2018   TU-1

038   SERIOUS DELINQUENCY, AND PUBLIC RECORD OR COLLECTED FIELD
013   TIME SINCE DELINQUENCY IS TOO RECENT OR UNKNOWN
016   LACK OF RECENT REVOLVING ACCOUNT INFORMATION
014   LENGTH OF TIME ACCOUNTS HAVE BEEN ESTABLISHED
INQUIRIES IMPACTED THE CREDIT SCORE

Score Information

Score Date: 06/26/2018   XPN-1

38	SERIOUS DELINQUENCY AND PUBLIC RECORD OR COLLECTED FIELD
18	NUMBER OF ACCOUNTS WITH DELINQUENCY
20	TIME SINCE DEROGATORY PUBLIC RECORD OR COLLECTION IS TOO SHORT
14	LENGTH OF TIME ACCOUNTS HAVE BEEN ESTABLISHED

Employment Information

Applicant

Employer: FLINT TROPICS
Position Held: Player
Start/Stop Dates: 01/01/05
Income: $42,000
Verified By/Date:

Co-Applicant

Employer:
Position Held:
Start/Stop Dates:
Income:
Verified By/Date:

Trade Information

Creditor Name	Date Reported		High Credit		Terms	Current Status		Historical Status			Past Due
Account Number	DLA	Date Opened	Credit Limit	Balance Owning	Acct. Type	ECOA	#Mo	Times Past Due			Last Past Due
								30	60	90	
ANY BANK	10/10	06/08	544	0		CHG OFF	99	1	1	3	
5225005784	06/18		30000		REV	1		XPN-1 TU-1 EFX-1			06/15

Late Dates: CHGOFF-06/2015 120+ SLOW05/2015 120 SLOW-04/2015 90 SLOW-03/2015 60 SLOW-2/2015 30 SLOW-01/2015
SETTLEMENT ACCEPTED ON THIS ACCOUNT
PAID CHARGE OFF
CREDIT CARD
BAD DEBT; PLACED FOR COLLECTION; SKIP
CHARGE OF AMOUNT IS 544

Collection Information

Creditor Name	Date Reported	Date Opened	High Credit	Balance	Acct. Type	Account Status	Past Due
Account Number	Client				Credit Limit	ECOA	Last Past Due
RIPOFF COLLECTIONS	04/18	06/18	1356	1356	I	CHG OFF	1356
198172694	MEDICAL PAYMENT DATA				1	XPN-1 TU-1 EFX-1	

DATE OF LAST ACTIVITY WITH ORIGINAL CREDITOR: 04/01/2018
HIGH CREDIT AMOUNT IS ORIGINAL LOAN AMOUNT
ACCOUNT SERIOUSLY PAST DUE DATE/ACCOUNT ASSIGNED TO ATTORNEY, COLLECTION AGENCY, OR CREDIT
GRANTOR'S INTERNAL COLLECTION DEPARTMENT
COLLECTION DEPARTMENT/AGENCY/ATTORNEY

UTILITY MEDICAL COLLECTION	09/17	08/17	207	207	I	CHG OFF	207
1212345646887	USA ELECTRIC-6				1	XPN-1	

HIGH CREDIT AMOUNT IS ORIGINAL LOAN AMOUNT
ACCOUNT SERIOUSLY PAST DUE DATE/ACCOUNT ASSIGNED TO ATTORNEY, COLLECTION AGENCY, OR CREDIT
GRANTOR'S INTERNAL COLLECTION DEPARTMENT
COLLECTION DEPARTMENT/AGENCY/ATTORNEY

Public Record Information

Public Record Type	Date Reported	Date Filed	Original Amount	Balance	Current Status	Amount Past Due
Case/Curt Number	Name					Segment

OBTAINED THROUGH TU, EFX and XPN

THE REPORTING BUREAU CERTIFIES THAT: public records have been checked for judgments, foreclosures, garnishments, bankruptcies, tax liens, and other legal actions involving the subject(s). Public Records were obtained directly through the repositories used, or by direct searches, or public records search firm other than the repository, or by all methods with the following results:

JUDGMENT	01/17	01/17		718		
001234567/1011048	STATE OF NEW YORK					XPN-1 EFX-1
QUEENS CITY REG COURT						
STATE TAX LIEN	01/11	01/11		718		
123456/298765						TU-1
RECORDER OF DEEDS						

Additional Employment Information

Current Employment - Applicant

Employer: FLINT TROPICS	Hire Date:	Date Discharged:
Employer: MAKING DONUTS	Hire Date:	Date Discharged:

Former Employment - Applicant

Employer: MOVIE STAR	Hire Date:	Date Discharged:

Additional Address Information

Current Addresses

1060 WEST ADDISON ST, CHICAGO, IL 60613	01/12/2017	TU-1

Former Addresses

1 NACHO HOUSE, BEVERLY HILLS, CA 90210		TU-1 XPN-1 EFX-1
123 MAIN STREET	06/01/2015	EFX-1 XPN-1 TU-1
14 JAMES BOND PLACE, CLEAVELAND, OH 44101	08/05/2013	XPN-1
1 EAST 161 ST. SMOOTT, BRONX, NY 10451	08/01/2011	EFX-1

Inquiries

In the last 120 days

DAVCO CREDIT SERVICES	06/26/2018	TU-1

Creditor Information List

Company	Phone	Address	City, State, Zip
ANY BANK	(800) 000-0000	P.O. BOX 1	WAUKEGAN, IL 60087
RIPOFF COLLECTIONS	(800) 000-0000	P.O. BOX 2	CAROL STREAM, IL 60197
UTILITY MEDICAL	(800) 000-0000	P.O. BOX 3	CAROL STREAM, IL 60197
QUEENS CNTY REG COURT	(718) 000-0000	P.O. BOX 4	JAMAICA, NY 11435

Creditor Information List

Company	Phone	Address	City, State, Zip
QUEENS COUNTY COURT	(718) 000-0000	P.O. BOX 1	WAUKEGAN, IL 60087

Source(s) of Information

File Segment	File Holder Name	Social Security #	Address
EFX-1	DOE, JOHN	012-34-5678	
TU-1	DOE, JOHN	012-34-5678	
XPN-1	DOE, JOHN	012-34-5678	

Alert and Validation

XPN OFAC ALERT   XPN-1
NAME DOES NOT MATCH OFAC/PLC LIST

ADDRESS DISCREPANCY   XPN-1 TU-1 EFX-1
THERE IS A SUBSTANTIAL DISCREPANCY BETWEEN THE ADDRESS ON INQUIRY INPUT AND THE ADDRESS(ES) ON FILE:

The Following AKA(s) Were Reported

Name	SS#	DOB	
DOE, JOHN			TU-1 EFX-1

Profile Summary

Credit History Summary

	Count	Balance	Payments	Past Due
Mortgage:	0	$0	$0	$0
Auto:	0	$0	$0	$0
Education:	0	$0	$0	$0
Installment:	0	$0	$0	$0
Open:	0	$0	$0	$0
Revolving:	2	$0	$0	$0
Other:	0	$0	$0	$0
Total:	2	$0	$0	$0
Secured Debt:	$0	$0	$0	$0
Unsecured Debt:	$0	$0	$0	$0

Derogatory Summary

	Count
Charge Offs:	1
Collections:	2
Incl. in Bankruptcy:	0
Late 30 Days:	1
Late 60 Days:	1
Late 90 Days:	3
Public Records:	2
Inquiries*:	1

* Number of inquiries within the last 120 days

Bureau Addresses

EQUIFAX	P.O. BOX 740241, ATLANTA, GA 30374	(800) 685-1111
EXPERIAN	P.O. BOX 2002, ALLEN, TX 75013	(888) 397-3742
TRANSUNION	2 BALDWIN PLACE, P.O. BOX 1000, CHESTER, PA 19022	(800) 888-4213

Notice: This is a merged report containing information supplied by the sources shown. The merge process is automated and the report may include some duplications and/or omissions.

This credit report is for the intended use of originating entity only. Use of this credit report by any other entity other than the originating entity constitutes second use. Second use users are required to post a secondary use inquiry on the consumer credit file. In addition, a Client Service Agreement must be completed and forwarded to the originating Credit Reporting Agency. Second use users can log onto the following website to post second use information and obtain a copy of the Client Service Agreement.

END OF REPORT - 06/26/2018 12:33:15 PM

Notes

Introduction: A Cautionary Tale

page

xi   *$8.4 trillion in mortgage debt:* "Consumer Credit Outstanding," Federalreserve.gov, February 7, 2017, accessed February 13, 2017, https://www.federalreserve.gov/releases/g19/current/default.htm.

       83 billion transactions: "Annual Report 2016," VISA Inc., p. 4, http://s1.q4cdn.com/050606653/files/doc_financials/annual/Visa-2016-Annual-Report.pdf.

       employed 234,000 people: "Annual Report 2015," J. P. Morgan Chase & Co., p. 1, https://www.jpmorganchase.com/corporate/investor-relations/document/2015-annualreport.pdf.

       completely different landscape: Thomas A. Durkin, "Credit Cards: Use and Consumer Attitudes, 1970–2000," *Federal Reserve Bulletin*, September 2000, p. 626, https://www.federalreserve.gov/pubs/Bulletin/2000/0900lead.pdf.

       The median home price: "Median and Average Sales Prices of New Homes Sold in United States: Annual Data," United States Census Bureau, accessed January 5, 2017, http://www.census.gov/const/uspriceann.pdf.

1. What You Don't Know Can Hurt You

4   *settled a class action lawsuit:* Summaries of the lawsuit settlements involving the three credit bureaus can be found here: *"White v. Experian Information Solutions," Lieff Cabraser Heimann & Bernstein Attorneys at Law* (blog), accessed December 12, 2016, https://www.lieffcabraser.com/consumer/credit-reporting; Laura Gunderson, "Equifax must pay $18.6 million after failing to fix Oregon woman's credit report," *The Oregonian*, July 26, 2013, accessed December 12, 2016, http://www.oregonlive.com/business/index.ssf/2013/07/equifax_must_pay_186_million_a.html; Jody Godoy, "Equifax Agrees to Remove Records and Pay $3M in FCRA Suit," Law360 (website), Decem-

ber 8, 2015, accessed December 12, 2016, https://www.law360.com
/articles/735629/equifax-agrees-to-remove-records-and-pay-3m-in
-fcra-suit.

2. What's in Your Score?

25 *just under 700:* "2016 State of Credit — Experian's Seventh Annual Credit Report," Experian.com, accessed January 5, 2017, http:
//www.experian.com/live-credit-smart/state-of-credit-2016.html.

3. Building the Perfect Credit Profile

37 *200,000 of its customers:* "Beyond Your Credit Score," Credit
Karma.com, last updated July 15, 2016, accessed January 5, 2017,
https://www.creditkarma.com/article/beyond_your_credit_score.

42 *90 days past due:* "2016 State of Credit — Experian's Seventh Annual Credit Report," Experian.com, accessed January 5, 2017, http:
//www.experian.com/live-credit-smart/state-of-credit-2016.html.
about 11 percent: "Official Cohort Default Rates for Schools,"
ED.gov, updated September 28, 2016, accessed October 1, 2016,
https://www2.ed.gov/offices/OSFAP/defaultmanagement/cdr.html.

43 *3 percent rate:* Andrew Haughwout, Donghoon Lee, Joelle Scally,
and Wilbert van der Klaauw, "Subprime Auto Debt Grows Despite
Rising Delinquencies," *Liberty Street Economics* (blog), November 30,
2016, accessed December 1, 2016, http://libertystreeteconomics.new
yorkfed.org/2016/11/just-released-subprime-auto-debt-grows-despite
-rising-delinquencies.html.

4. Gaming the System

55 *In July 2017:* Stacy Cowley, "Your Credit Score May Soon Look Better," *New York Times,* June 26, 2017, https://www.nytimes.com
/2017/06/26/business/dealbook/your-credit-score-may-soon-look
-better.html.

62 *A 2016 study:* Liz Hamel, Mira Norton, Karen Pollitz, Larry Lev-
itt, Gary Claxton, and Mollyann Brodie, "The Burden of Medical Debt:
Results from the Kaiser Family Foundation/New York Times Medical
Bills Survey," The Henry J. Kaiser Family Foundation (website), January 5, 2016, accessed December 1, 2016, http://kff.org/report-section
/the-burden-of-medical-debt-introduction.

6. Preparing Your Credit Score for a New Home Purchase

80 *the average income:* U.S. Department of Commerce: Bureau of
Economic Analysis, "Per Capita Personal Income," *Infoplease*, accessed

February 2, 2017, http://www.infoplease.com/ipa/A0104547.html; Tami Luhby, "The Middle Class Gets a Big Raise ... Finally!", *CNN Money*, September 13, 2016, accessed February 2, 2017, http://money .cnn.com/2016/09/13/news/economy/median-income-census.

got from a relative: "Median Sales Price for New Houses Sold in the United States," FRED Economic Data, Federal Reserve Bank of St. Louis (website), updated February 24, 2017, accessed March 1, 2017, https://fred.stlouisfed.org/series/MSPNHSUS.

81 *applications are rejected:* "HAMP Application Outcome Summary, as of April 2015," Treasury HAMP Data, accessed June 5, 2015, quoted in Ruth Mantell, "72% of struggling borrowers rejected from federal mortgage-assistance program," *MarketWatch*, July 30, 2015, accessed March 1, 2017, http://www.marketwatch.com/story/72-of -struggling-borrowers-rejected-from-federal-mortgage-assistance -program-2015-07-29.

7. The Care and Feeding of Credit Cards

97 *In 2015, Experian:* Fred O. Williams, "How much is the average credit card debt in America?", Creditcards.com, updated January 18, 2017, accessed February 2, 2017, http://www.creditcards.com/credit -card-news/average-credit-card-debt.php.

100 *to their best customers:* "Average interest charged by commercial banks on credit cards 1974–present," Federal Reserve Statistical Release, St. Louis Fed, quoted in Tim Chen, "Historical Credit Card Interest Rates," *NerdWallet*, accessed March 1, 2017, https://www.nerdwal let.com/blog/credit-card-data/historical-credit-card-interest-rates.

8. Protecting Your Credit Score from Identity Theft

111 *had been compromised:* Vindu Goel and Nicole Perlroth, "Yahoo Says 1 Billion User Accounts Were Hacked," *New York Times*, December 14, 2016, accessed December 14, 2016, https://www.nytimes .com/2016/12/14/technology/yahoo-hack.html.

113 *five years of hard time:* "Federal Mandatory Minimums," Families Against Mandatory Minimums, accessed December 5, 2016, http:// famm.org/wp-content/uploads/2013/08/Chart-All-Fed-MMs-NW.pdf.

114 *almost twenty million people:* Erika Harrell, "Victims of Identity Theft, 2014," US Department of Justice Bulletin, September 2015, quoted in Cody Gredler, "The Real Cost of Identity Theft," CSID — A Part of Experian (website), accessed December 5, 2016, https://www .csid.com/2016/09/real-cost-identity-theft.

121 *more than 60 percent:* Christina Lamontagne, "NerdWallet Health finds medical bankruptcy accounts for majority of personal bankrupt-

cies," *NerdWallet,* June 19, 2013, accessed March 1, 2017, https://www
.nerdwallet.com/blog/health/managing-medical-bills/nerdwallet
-health-study-estimates-56-million-americans-65-struggle-medical
-bills-2013-2.

10. Higher Education: Navigating the School Loan Landscape

148 *more than $1.5* trillion: Federal Reserve Board of Governors,
"Consumer Credit Outstanding," Federalreserve.gov, February 7, 2017,
accessed February 13, 2017, https://www.federalreserve.gov/releases
/g19/current/default.htm.

149 *$31,000 in student debt:* Katie Lobosco, "Students are graduat-
ing with $30,000 in student loans," *CNN Money,* October 18, 2016, ac-
cessed December 5, 2016, http://money.cnn.com/2016/10/18/pf/college
/average-student-loan-debt.

150 *price on an average year of college:* "Average Published Undergraduate Charges by Sector, 2016–17," Collegeboard.org, accessed March
1, 2017, https://trends.collegeboard.org/college-pricing/figures-tables
/average-published-undergraduate-charges-sector-2016-17.

Index

Index

28% M/T (Max)   23 H Value

of gross income   × 28 %

$$\begin{array}{r} 23 \\ \times\ 28\% \\ \hline 184 \\ 46 \\ \hline 644 \end{array}$$

$$\begin{array}{r} 450 \\ 4\,\overline{)1800}\,/\text{mo. mort} \end{array}$$

$$\begin{array}{r} 1800 \\ \times 4 \\ \hline 7,200 \end{array}$$

$$\begin{array}{r} 7,200 \\ 1\,800 \\ \hline 5,400 \end{array}$$

$$\begin{array}{r} 1700\,/\text{wk gross} \\ 4\,\overline{)5400} \\ 4 \\ \hline 14 \end{array}$$

$$\begin{array}{r} 42.20 \\ 4020\,/\text{hr.} \\ 40\,\overline{)1700} \\ 16 \\ \hline 100 \end{array}$$

Pg. ⑧1 , 82, 83, 85, ⑧6 , -87, 90, 93,

181, 182,